HOW TO MAKE

Pottery

HOW TO MAKE

Pottery

AND OTHER CERAMIC WARE

BY

MURIEL PARGH TUROFF

ILLUSTRATED BY
THE AUTHOR

GRAMERCY PUBLISHING COMPANY • NEW YORK

This edition published by Gramercy Publishing Company,
a division of Crown Publishers, Inc.
a b c d e f g h

*To my mother and
to people everywhere,
for more creative living.*

Contents

Chapter Three

Chapter Four

Chapter Four (Cont'd)

Chapter Five

Chapter Six

Chapter Seven

Chapter Eight

Chapter Nine

Chapter Ten

Chapter Eleven

Appendices

HOW TO MAKE

Pottery

Introduction

OUR PEOPLE are coming of age in their awareness of the beauty of ceramics in the home and garden. They are learning how simple and fascinating it can be as a hobby craft. In small towns, in large cities, people everywhere are asking, "Where can I learn to make pottery? How can I make figurines?"

Classes and craftsmen's groups are coming into existence throughout the country. They are made up of people in all occupations and walks of life. Many are impelled by sheer love of the feel of clay in their fingers, and by the joy of watching a piece of earth take on a beautiful form as they work. Some become interested because of a particular object they want to make for decoration or use in the home. Sometimes it is a gift they want to create for a loved one; such a gift would be unique in its personal expression and therefore would have a preciousness which cannot be purchased in any shop, at any price.

There are some who would like to make ceramic objects, but are too timid to try because they were never skillful at any art work. There is no reason for such fear. While art training is a help, it is not essential. In fact, in some cases, it is an advantage to have had no training, especially for those who soon find that they are evolving a naïve, personal way of expressing ideas.

The teacher of ceramics is always interested in knowing why people want to learn. What are the values derived? Why is it that even those busily engaged in their everyday work or professions make certain to reserve some time, if only an hour or two per week, for this craft?

There was the middle-aged man who worked in a factory during the day. He felt that his work with clay was the best way of expressing things within him which he had no opportunity to express while he was busy earning his livelihood. His first entrance into the ceramics class was with great timidity. "But I can't do this. I was never an artist!" With a little encouragement and guidance, however, he was soon amazed at the beautiful things he created.

A young woman who did secretarial work in the daytime came to ceramics class in the evening. She felt the need of this outlet for her creative energies, and was able to approach her day's work with more freshness and enthusiasm because of it.

There were several housewives, busy with the cares of home and children, who came to class with great eagerness. Often they said that this was the only thing they did during the week which enabled them to relax. Some of them made nursery rhyme characters for their children; others shaped handsome pieces of pottery, such as ash trays, candlesticks, dishes, pitchers, a specially designed bowl to harmonize

1

with certain furnishings, or vases for flowers and table decorations. Some were intrigued with the lovely ceramic jewelry they themselves were able to create.

Usually the children caught the enthusiasm from the mothers and they started coming to class. At one time, a college professor and his wife and son attended the classes. Today, in a number of homes, ceramics is becoming a family hobby.

Among my students in the Veterans Administration Hospital was a man who was being given physiotherapy for a paralyzed hand. He was certain, in spite of the doctors' opinion to the contrary, that he would never be able to move his fingers again. With his good hand he began to work in clay and and he made a handsome set of ceramic checkers. He became so intrigued with his work that before long he was using the fingers of his paralyzed hand without even being aware of it.

In general, Americans seem to be entering an era of more intimate relationship with the objects surrounding their daily living. Perhaps we are at last feeling the impact of the machine age and reacting against the stultifying influence of cheap mass production upon the nation's aesthetic taste. Forward-thinking manufacturers recognize this fact and more and more are using the talents of fine artists and designers.

Contemporary Americans are learning to recapture some of the personal charm of living as practiced by Pennsylvania Dutch settlers of early eighteenth century. In those days, a Dutch mother would have the potter make a special plate for each member in the family. These plates were handed down as keepsakes from one generation to the next. They were often designed with beautiful birds, fruits and flowers, with proverbs, quaint sayings, or pictures commemorating some special event in their lives. They are a true reflection of a people's folkways. Some of these plates have since found their way into museums; some are valued pieces in the hands of ardent collectors and others are precious today as family heirlooms.

Many museums are today encouraging the craftsman to take his rightful place beside the artist as one who contributes an integral part to the creative expression of his time.

Outstanding in this respect is the Syracuse Museum of Fine Arts which seventeen years ago established the first national ceramic show in this country to encourage the creation of American ceramics. The exhibitions were suspended during the war years, but were resumed with greater success than ever in 1946. Under the able leadership of the museum's director, Anna Wetherill Olmsted, the museum held its thirteenth annual exhibition in November, 1948. Each year, the museum buys something from these shows. It now has a collection of the finest in American ceramics.

The Cleveland Museum of Art is unique in the way it provides a dynamic force of integration between work produced by living artists and craftsmen on the one hand, and an appreciative, buying public on the other. Through his understanding and enthusiasm, William Milliken, the director of the museum, has educated the public to the value of fine art and crafts in the home. The annual May show at this museum features various arts and crafts done by Clevelanders. That ceramics has become a major craft is attested by the fact that in 1919, at the first May show, no ceramics were represented. In 1946, one hundred and seventy pieces were exhibited and of these ninety-one were sold.

The people of Cleveland look forward to this annual event which they attend in great numbers. In 1948, $22,000.00 worth of paintings, sculptures and crafts were sold. Many ceramic pieces were among them.

This museum proudly exhibits its beautiful collection of contemporary American ceramics beside its collection of the ancients.

The fine job of education and integration done by the Cleveland Museum may well be used as a model by other museums. They should not content themselves with being storage houses for antiques, but rather serve as a means of relating the past to all that is alive today.

Today's antique was once someone's dream brought to life by a pair of loving hands. The things made by craftsmen and hobbyists reflect contemporary thoughts and modes of living. Many such creations will become the treasured Americana of tomorrow.

For those who wish to devote their lives to ceramics as a career, there are a number of good professional schools and universities which offer this training. There are also many highly technical books on the subject. This book, however, will deal with the special needs and problems of the beginner.

It will endeavor to guide those who study in a group under the direction of a teacher as well as those who pioneer for themselves; and equally those who prefer to purchase supplies ready for use from the many fine ceramic supply companies in existence; or those who enjoy the rugged satisfaction of preparing their own materials.

Thanks and Acknowledgments

To Eda Rogers and Sam Zagat whose encouragement and guidance stimulated me to write this book.

To Zan S. Zobel and James Perlowin of Perlowin Studios for their kind assistance in the art work.

To Florence Fishbein Kuper of Henry Street Settlement, N. Y., who posed her hands for the illustrations of the pottery wheel technique.

To the following for their kind assistance in the chapter on Occupational Therapy:

Anthony Aliverti, Instructor of the blind, Veterans Administration Hospital, Bronx, N. Y.

Helen Applebaum, O.T.R., Veterans Administration Hospital, Bronx, N. Y.

Theresa Nova Bader, Instructor of the blind at the N. Y. Guild for the Jewish Blind.

Edith H. Brokaw, Instructor of Occupational Therapy courses, College of Physicians and Surgeons, Columbia University.

Virginia Nowicki, Director of Occupational Therapy, Institute of Rehabilitation, New York University.

Eva M. Otto, Educational Field Secretary, American Occupational Therapy Association.

Ruth M. Rumsey, Assistant Chief, Occupational Therapy Section Veterans Administration Hospital, Bronx, N. Y.

Wilma L. West, Executive Director of the American Occupational Therapy Association.

To John Marquis, Assistant Director of Research for Glazes, Pemco Corporation, Baltimore, Md. for glaze formulas 1 to 4.

To H. C. Tucker of the Ferro Enamel Corporation, Allied Engineering Division, Cleveland, O. for glaze formulas 5 to 7.

To Ceramic Industry, Chicago, Ill. for glaze formula 4.

To Prof. A. Hyatt Verrill, archaeologist, for permission to illustrate the prehistoric pottery he found in the ruins at Coclé, Panama.

To A. Calavas of Librairie des Arts Décoratifs, Paris, France, for permission to use the illustrations of the Cretan pottery.

To all the museums mentioned in the Design chapter for their kind cooperation.

The electric kiln described on page 65 was used in the ceramics classes at Denver University during the summer of 1942. Plans were originated by Frank W. Smith.

CHAPTER ONE

Materials, Tools and Equipment

Except for the pottery wheel and kiln, the tools required for the making of ceramics are simple and inexpensive. Some of them can be made at home. Some can be found in the average kitchen, workshop, or hardware store.

This book describes many methods of forming objects by hand without the aid of a pottery wheel. The wheel, therefore, is not indispensable. If it can be afforded, it is desirable and can be obtained from most supply houses. (See chapter on sources of supplies.) Where it is not feasible for an individual to buy a wheel, it might possibly be bought through the concerted efforts of a group who may have the use of a workshop in a "Y," settlement house, community center, or someone's basement. The same conditions apply to the purchase of a kiln. Small electric kilns may be purchased within the range of $25 to about $65.

All the materials mentioned in this chapter are obtained from supply houses. The materials come in powdered form, with the exceptions of sodium silicate, glycerin, and gum tragacanth.

For Preparation of Clay

Equipment:

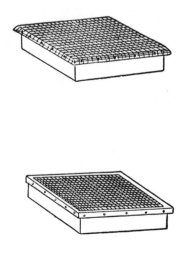

1. Screen—sold by supply houses. Can be made at home easily with 16" square of copper (because it is non-rusting) window screening, about 60 mesh. Nail screening to a wooden frame 12" square, 4" deep, ¾" thick. Reinforce with 1" molding on the outside edges.

2. An old coffee grinder or coarse meat grinder.

3. Plaster bowl—cast 1½" thickness of plaster over an inverted mixing bowl. (See p. 45 for directions for casting.)

7

4. Wedging board—Half the surface of the illustrated board is made of wood, the other half is plaster. If clay is just right, it is wedged on the wood; if too damp, it is wedged on the plaster. Boards of this type can be purchased from ceramic supply companies, or may be homemade.

The wedging table illustrated here is also simple to make. The table is made into a box 6″ deep of ⅞″ finished wood. It has a wooden board bottom. Cover bottom of box with stones or gravel 2″ deep. Pour a solid mass of plaster or cement over the gravel till it is level with the top of the box. The legs are made of 4 x 4 posts. The shelf under the table reinforces it and provides space for storing bats, bowls, molds, etc. The wire used for cutting clay should be tightly strung and made of heavy non-rusting wire such as copper or stainless steel.

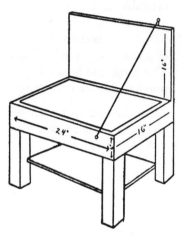

MATERIALS:

1. Sodium silicate (water glass) sold in any hardware store.
2. Sodium carbonate.
3. Flint, 5 lbs.
4. Ball clay, 5 lbs.
5. China clay (kaolin), 5 lbs.

For Forming

EQUIPMENT:

1. Modeling tools, 2 or 3 different sizes. One should have wire ends.
2. A small, smooth, fine-grained elephant's-ear sponge, sold by pottery supply companies.
3. 2 or 3 plaster bats. These are made very simply by casting plaster 1″ to 1½″ thick in a

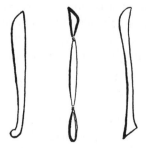

pie tin. It is handy to form an object on a round bat because it can be revolved easily as the piece is being shaped.

4. An inexpensive, medium sized brush for applying slip at joinings.

5. 2 or 3 flexible steel scrapers for smoothing leather-hard or bone-dry ware; may be home-made or bought from a supply house.

6. Rolling pin or an 18″ length of 1″ doweling.

7. Paring knife.

8. Piece of oilcloth 18″ x 18″.

MATERIALS:

1. Clay.
2. Slip.
3. Grog.

For Decorating

EQUIPMENT:

1. A sprayer (flit gun or vacuum cleaner attachment).

2. Slip tracer (small rubber bulb with a nozzle).

3. 8″ square of glass for grinding underglaze.

4. A small strainer such as used in the kitchen.

5. 2 or 3 camel's hair brushes of different sizes. One brush should be very fine for drawing lines.

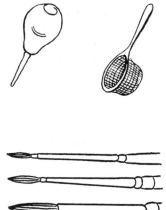

MATERIALS:

1. Engobe.
2. 8 oz. glycerin.
3. Underglaze, several colors, ¼ lb. each.
4. ⅛ lb. gum tragacanth.

For Glazing

Supply companies listed at the end of this book are able to supply the student with a wide range of glazes in many variations of colors and texture. It is wise, for those who wish to buy their materials, to order clay, engobe, and glaze from the same house and to specify that all three "fit," *i.e.*, have the same amount of shrinkage and mature at the same temperature. These glazes are ready to be used with the addition of water. 1 lb. of glaze of any color goes a long way.

For those who prefer to mix their own glazes, the following equipment is necessary:

1. A pair of gram scales.

2. A 10 oz. and a 32 oz. mortar and pestle.

3. An 80 mesh screen.

4. 2 or 3 inexpensive flat brushes of different sizes for applying glaze to the ware.

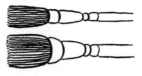

5. A grinding wheel for grinding off glaze which may have dripped down on the foot of the ware; also for grinding and sharpening tools.

MATERIALS:

1. 1 lb. bentonite.

2. 5 lbs. frit (see chapter on glazing).

3. Colorants 4 oz. each:
>   Antimony
>   Copper Carbonate
>   Cobalt oxide
>   Chrome
>   Iron oxide
>   Iron chromate
>   Manganese oxide
>   Nickel
>   Rutile
>   Titanium Oxide
>   Uranium Oxide

4. China clay (kaolin).

5. Flint.

For Firing

1. Kiln.
2. Shelves and props.
3. Stilts for stacking ware.
4. Pyrometric cones (see chapter on firing).

For Mold-making and Casting

EQUIPMENT:

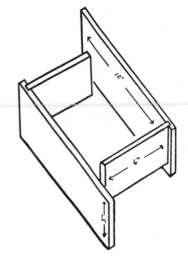

1. 3 or 4 wooden wedges.
2. Heavy twine.
3. 2 or 3 enamel basins or mixing bowls.
4. Strip of linoleum or corrugated board. Size depends upon the size of the mold to be made. These are used to form a cottle (retaining wall for a mold; see p. 45).
5. A box adjustable to various sizes makes an excellent cottle. It is made as follows: Use ⅞" finished wood. Make two wooden angles as in the illustration. When adjusted to the desired size box, the angles are tied together with twine and all the seams are sealed with soft clay.

MATERIALS:

1. Cornstarch 1 lb.
2. Plaster—10 to 15 lbs. of U. S. Gypsum Pottery Plaster or Molding Plaster #1. Dry plaster absorbs moisture which renders it unfit for use. Plaster should, therefore, be stored in a covered container and kept in a dry place.
3. Separator—New plaster will adhere to a surface of other plaster. (It adheres also to many other types of surfaces.) To separate one piece of plaster from the other as in a two-piece mold, a "separator" is applied between the pieces. Separator seals the pores of the surface so that adhesion is prevented. A good separator is made as follows:

   a. Grate 1 bar castile soap. Simmer in 1 qt. water until dissolved.

   b. Stir in ½ cup paraffin. Continue to simmer to the consistency of syrup.

   c. Place in a covered jar, where it will keep indefinitely.

For Throwing on the Wheel

EQUIPMENT:

1. A kick wheel or electric wheel. The former is revolved by foot motion and the latter by electricity. The latter preferably should have a variable speed control instead of a single speed. Both types of wheels should revolve counterclockwise.

2. Two or three turning tools. These may be purchased or made from strips of sheet metal, ½″ to 1″ wide, 8″ long. Ends should be bent at a right angle about ¾″ down and they should be sharpened by grinding.

3. About 2 ft. of copper or stainless steel wire for removing ware from the wheel. Attach a stick to each end of the wire to form a pair of handles.

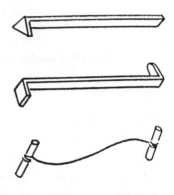

It is wise to clean up and put things away as one goes along in the process of his work. A clean workroom is very conducive to the making of beautiful things.

CHAPTER TWO

How to Make Clay Behave

It is essential that the student have a knowledge of different types of clay and what these clays will or will not do. Once the student learns the characteristics of clay, he will find it easy to work with it instead of against it. Then will he get the best results.

Plasteline is clay mixed with glycerine or some oily base to prevent the clay from drying out. Plasteline is good to use for models from which to make molds, or for sculpture which is going to be reproduced. It is not fit for anything which is to be fired in a kiln.

Among commercial clays some are self-hardening and others require so little heat that they can be fired in a kitchen oven. Such clays are not satisfactory for ceramics.

Ceramic clay may be classified into three main groups: earthenware, stoneware and porcelain. Earthenware, which is found in various colors, has a low maturing point (from 1740° to about 2100° Fahrenheit). It fires opaque and will absorb water. Stoneware is also opaque but has little or no porosity. Its maturing temperature is between 2200° and 2400° F. Both earthenware and stoneware are well suited to strong, virile-looking forms. Porcelain and china require up to 2600° F. to mature. They are white, translucent, delicate in character and have hardly any porosity at all. Porcelain clay is not very plastic, which makes it difficult to model or throw on the pottery wheel. It is usually cast. Stoneware and porcelain are clay mixtures which must be prepared. Earthenware is generally found in its natural state.

Some students find great satisfaction in digging from the earth the clay for their creations. To be completely responsible for the transformation of this humble material into an object of beauty and utility is a special joy known only to those who have done it.

Clay is decomposed feldspathic rock. There is an abundance of it all over the earth. One may be fortunate enough to find it in one's back yard.

To test whether it is clay, pick up a bit of it and wet it. If it is plastic and sticky enough to form a smooth ball, it is clay.

Clay dug out of the earth may vary in color and texture, depending upon the locale where it is found and its mineral composition. Some clays may be too plastic (pliant), thus making it impossible to build a form which would hold its shape. Such clay usually feels rich and fatty to the touch. Some clay may not be plastic enough. Such clay cracks easily while being shaped. Its particles do not bind together very well and appear somewhat crumbly. Such clay is called "short." A clay of good working quality must be plastic enough to shape and firm enough to hold its form.

When the beginner selects clay whose firing does not exceed cone 03 (see pp. 19, 20, and 21 on cones and temperatures), he will get the best results by using the earthenware group of clays as follows:

For jewelry and other delicate forms—white clay which has strength and is very plastic.

For pottery—any of the earthenware clays. Mix with fine grog for the large pieces. (See page 15.)

For tiles—clay mixed with 20% to 25% grog.

For sculpture—any of the earthenware clays for small figurines. Mix with 25% grog for large pieces. Red or brown clay gives a pleasing effect if the piece is to remain unglazed.

How to Process Clay

1. Remove impurities such as twigs, leaves, roots, and large stones.

2. Dry the chunks of clay in the sun if possible.

3. Break up the dry chunks and put them through an old coffee grinder or coarse meat grinder.

4. Fill half a galvanized pail with warm water.

5. Add ground clay till there is a mound above the water. Do not stir.

6. Let mixture stand 24 hours; then stir and sieve through a 60 mesh copper screen. This removes the impurities and breaks up the lumps. Allow to stand another 24 hours and then remove water that may collect on top.

7. Put about a cupful of slip (the name for liquid clay) into a plaster bowl. The plaster absorbs the water, thus stiffening the slip into clay. When clay is stiff enough, shape and bend it. If it is "short," cracks will appear. When that happens, add to the mixture up to 7% bentonite or up to 10% ball clay. This makes the clay more plastic. If clay is too plastic, add some flint.

8. After slip has been adjusted (if necessary) as described above, pour it into a plaster bowl to stiffen it into clay.

How to Store Clay

Clay is best stored in a tightly covered container which will not rust. A covered stoneware crock or a galvanized metal garbage can is good. If the latter is used, put a couple of bricks into the bottom, and a wooden board or plaster bat on the bricks. The clay should rest on the board or bat. This permits about 2″ of water to be kept in the bottom of the can without having the clay immersed in the water. Keep tightly covered. Add water from time to time. Thus, the clay is kept in a moist, plastic state, ready for use. Clay may be stored moist indefinitely; the longer, the better. The ancient Chinese potters took pride in storing clay for the next generation to use.

Keep clay and container free from foreign bodies, such as bits of plaster, hair, bristles, threads, paper, etc. Such matter imbedded in the clay may cause the piece to crack or break in the firing.

Clay Color

Clay may be found in several colors, including black, white, ochre, blue, red, grey, or buff. The color of the raw clay is not always the same after it has been fired. It is wise to test-fire a sample of the clay so that its biscuit (first unglazed firing) color may be determined. This varies with the degree of heat to which the clay was fired. For example, raw clay which is grey may become pale pink at about 1800° F. and pale buff at about 1900° F.

Shrinkage

Clay shrinks as it dries. It shrinks still more in the firing. Some clays shrink more than others. The approximate amount is about 10%. When test-firing a sample of clay for color and texture, it is also wise to measure the sample before and after firing so that the amount of shrinkage may be determined. A good sample is a slab 5" x 2" x ¼" thick.

Shrinkage may be decreased by adding flint or grog to the clay. Grog is clay that has been biscuit-fired and then crushed. Some people prepare their own grog from broken biscuit-fired pieces. It can be bought at very little cost at any supply company in varying degrees of fineness. The coarser the particles of grog added to the clay, the coarser the texture of the fired object will be. 60 mesh grog makes a good clay mixture for sculpture larger than 10 inches. For small figurines use a finer grog.

Grog makes clay porous and is used for objects which are not intended to hold water. Grog also prevents warpage and is, therefore, very useful for tile making and for sculpture. 20% is a good proportion of grog in a clay mixture.

Purchasing Clay

Those who prefer prepared clay can buy it from supply houses in many parts of the country. The clay is already processed and cleaned. It is sold in various colors, in moist or dry form. If moist, it is ready for use. If dry, it comes in powdered form and has to be mixed with water to be made into slip from which the plastic clay is formed as described below.

Slip

There are several uses for slip in ceramics. They are:

1. Slip for casting:

a. Fill half a 3 or 4 gallon crock or galvanized pail with warm water.

b. Add enough dry powdered clay till a small mound appears on top of the water. Do not stir. Let it stand 24 hours.

c. Sieve it through a screen. This breaks up all the lumps. Leave it for another 24 hours.

d. If there is any water on top at the end of that period, remove it.

e. Add about 1/16 teaspoonful of sodium silicate (water glass) and 1/16 teaspoonful of sodium carbonate. Potters call these "deflocculents." The chemical action of deflocculents causes the slip to remain in suspension and maintain a smooth, creamy consistency. The slip should weigh about 26 oz. per pint. If it weighs more, it needs more water; if less, it contains too much water. Stir well.

f. Store slip in a tightly covered rust-proof container.

2. Slip for making plastic clay:

a. Follow directions above up to and including "d."

b. Pour slip into a plaster bowl to stiffen it. Never use sodium silicate or sodium carbonate in slip which is to be made into plastic clay because this makes the clay short and renders it unfit for modeling.

3. Slip for adhesive purposes:

(Slip acts as a binder between one piece of clay and another. It is, therefore, useful in attaching handles to cups, limbs to figures, etc.)

a. Using a rolling pin, roll a lump of clay about the size of an orange into a slab about 1/4" thick. Let it dry thoroughly (allow about two days).

b. Break slab into a jar with enough warm water in it to slightly more than cover the clay. The clay will soften and become slip. The slip should be of a heavy cream consistency. Slip made from dried clay has greater adhesive properties.

c. Keep covered. Water may be added if slip becomes too thick. Stir well before using.

4. Engobe:

Slip that is used for decoration is called "engobe." (See chapter on decoration.) It should be made of the same clay as the body to be decorated, because it is important that the body and engobe have the same amount of shrinkage.

Engobe is best applied when the body is almost leather-hard. (When clay is still wet but too stiff to be bent, it is called "leather-hard.") In this state, the body has already shrunk somewhat. The engobe, therefore, has to be adjusted for an equal amount of shrinkage. This is done as follows:

Use slip which becomes white or light buff after biscuit-firing. Add 25% flint and 10% feldspar. (If engobe peels away from the body after firing, it is an indication that the body shrank more than the engobe. Add a little ball clay to the engobe to correct this. If engobe shows cracks after firing, it shrank more than the body. To correct this, add more flint.)

Colored Engobes

Red is made simply by using slip made of red clay and adding flint and feldspar as above. The following colors may be obtained by adding colorants to the light-colored engobe (preferably white):

black:	5% each of iron, chrome, and manganese oxides.
white:	10% tin oxide.
pink, brown, purple:	up to 8% manganese oxide.
yellow:	10% antimony with 1% iron oxide.
yellow:	5 to 8% vanadium stain.
olive green:	up to 6% chromium oxide.
ivory:	up to 10% rutile.
green:	up to 5% copper carbonate.
blue:	¼ to ½% cobalt (this is very strong in color).
brown:	4 to 10% iron oxide.
purple-brown:	5 to 8% manganese carbonate.
grey:	5 to 10% iron chromate.

Ceramic supply companies are now selling body stains which are used instead of oxides to make colored slip for casting or decorating. They come in a variety of colors and are mixed into the slip in the same manner as the oxides.

The best way to mix a colorant into engobe is to grind it well in a small mortar and pestle with just enough engobe to make a thick paste. Add the thoroughly ground paste to the rest of the engobe. Mix well for uniform color.

Purchasing Engobe

The student who prefers to buy engobes ready for use can find them in most ceramic supply houses. The engobes come in a number of fine colors. It is best to use clay from the same company and to specify, when ordering, that the engobe fit the clay. Some supply houses sell engobes which are adjusted for use on bone-dry ware.

How to Salvage Old Clay

Old, dried-out pieces of clay should be converted to slip by soaking in water in a rust-proof, covered container free from foreign matter. To make plastic clay, put slip through a screen. Pour into a plaster bowl to stiffen. Store in the clay container when plastic enough for forming.

Drying of Ware

Ware must never be set into a kiln before it is bone-dry. A piece that still has moisture in it will crack or break in the firing. Do not dry ware in a draft. Weather and humidity affect the drying of clay because it absorbs moisture from the air. Small, thin pieces dry quickly. Large, heavy pieces must be dried slowly and with care, as follows:

1. A piece of newspaper or paper toweling should be spread under a large piece of ware. The weight of such pieces puts a strain on the shrinking process. The soft paper under the piece enables it to slide smoothly along with the contraction, thus preventing possible cracks.

2. Put a damp cloth on the rim or any other part of the piece which is likely to dry more quickly than the rest. It is important that every part of the ware dry uniformly throughout.

3. The drying of large pieces must be retarded with slightly damp cloths in the first stages. Rapid drying causes cracks. The larger and heavier the piece, the longer it should be allowed to dry.

4. After four or five days of slow drying, the piece may be placed in the sun, over a radiator or other mildly warm spot for final, thorough drying. At this stage it is advisable to invert the piece to insure all around air circulation.

5. Flat ware such as plates or tiles should be dried in a horizontal position to prevent strain and warpage.

Keeping Ware Damp

One does not often finish ceramic sculpture or large pieces of pottery in one day. Since clay has to be kept moist throughout the working stage, wrap work in a damp cloth. The size of the cloth and the amount of moisture in it should depend upon the size of the piece and how long it will be before work can be resumed. If an interval of several days or more will elapse, wrap piece closely in a damp cloth and cover completely with oilcloth or rubber sheet. When putting any sort of damp wrappings on the ware, care should be taken not to make the cloth too wet or the clay will become so saturated with water that it will collapse. In wrapping, also take care that no heavy weight be placed on any delicate part of the figure.

Another effective way of keeping work damp is to place it in a covered, airtight box; or to invert a large metal can over the piece. An old-fashioned zinc-lined icebox makes a perfect damp closet.

Mending Green Ware

Scrape some clay with sandpaper or a knife from the bottom of the dried ware. Mix it with the slip of the same clay and wedge the mixture tightly into the crack with a brush or modeling tool.

If the piece has a clean break it can be mended by making the pieces slowly and uniformly moist to the leather-hard stage by proper wrapping with moist rags and oilcloth. Then mend the broken pieces with thick slip. If the piece is badly broken, it cannot be mended.

Mending Biscuit-ware

A crack in biscuit-ware may be filled in with a thick paste made of finely ground grog and sodium silicate (water glass).

Cones

Pyrometric cones are pyramidal pieces of clay. They are made of mixtures of clay accurately designed to withstand varying temperatures of heat. Each cone bears a number to indicate the degree of heat at which it will bend over. Cone 1, for instance, is made so that it bends at 2057° F. As the numbers increase (cone 2, 3, 4, etc.), the temperature tolerance increases. Temperatures decrease with cone 01, 02, 03, etc., all the way down to 050. Cones will not react properly to rapid heating. Most cones are intended to be used in a clear atmosphere inside the kiln For reduction firing, specially designed cones may be ordered. The cone, therefore, is a measure of the combination of time, temperature and atmosphere in the kiln. The cone is imbedded in a bit of soft clay mixed with grog and is placed in that part of the kiln where it can be seen through the peephole. When the temperature of the kiln approaches the maturing point of the cone, it begins to bend. When maturity is reached, the top of the cone is bent over to the level of its base. When temperature has gone beyond the maturing point, the cone is completely collapsed because it has begun to melt. When placing the cone, it should be tilted slightly to the side where it would not be likely to touch the ware when the cone starts bending. The cone provides an inexpensive, sufficiently accurate temperature gauge to the potter who has no mechanical heat indicator on his kiln.*

Temperature

When clay is fired to maturity, it becomes hard, strong and dense. That is called "vitrification." Some clays mature, or vitrify, at higher temperatures than others. When clay is overfired, it darkens in color. When it is overfired too much, it melts, thus causing the object to collapse. When clay is underfired, it is very porous and water will seep through it. It is also brittle and easily broken. When firing a sample of clay, therefore, it is important to observe the temperature at which it has been fired, and how porous or dense the fired sample has become. A simple test is to put a little water on the fired piece. If the water disappears rapidly, the piece has not been fired long enough. Also, when struck lightly it makes a dull sound. A well-fired piece of clay should feel strong and dense, and have a clear ring when struck.

* The Edward Orton, Jr., Ceramic Foundation, 1445 Summit Street, Columbus, Ohio, will send upon request their very excellent booklet, *The Properties and Uses of Pyrometric Cones.*

When clay is ordered from a supply house, the desired maturing temperature should be specified. This should be limited to the maximum temperature at which one's kiln is able to operate. A good range for the amateur to work with is from cone 06 to cone 03 (1841° to 1976° Fahrenheit). Clay dug out of the earth, cleaned and processed, should be test-fired first at cone 06, then at 05, 04 and 03 to see which gives the best results.

TEMPERATURE EQUIVALENTS OF CONES

CONE	°CENT	°FAHR	CONE	°CENT	°FAHR	CONE	°CENT	°FAHR	CONE	°CENT	°FAHR
022	585	1085	06	1005	1841	10	1260	2300	29	1640	2984
021	595	1103	05	1030	1886	11	1285	2345	30	1650	3002
020	625	1157	04	1050	1922	12	1310	2390	31	1680	3056
019	630	1166	03	1080	1976	13	1350	2462	32	1700	3092
018	670	1238	02	1095	2003	14	1390	2534	32½	1725	3137
017	720	1328	01	1110	2030	15	1410	2570	33	1745	3173
016	735	1355	1	1125	2057	16	1450	2642	34	1760	3200
015	770	1418	2	1135	2075	17	1465	2669	35	1785	3245
014	795	1463	3	1145	2093	18	1485	2705	36	1810	3290
013	825	1517	4	1165	2129	19	1515	2759	37	1820	3308
012	840	1544	5	1180	2156	20	1520	2768	38	1835	3335
011	875	1607	6	1190	2174	23	1580	2876	39	1865	3389
010	890	1634	7	1210	2210	26	1595	2903	40	1885	3425
09	930	1706	8	1225	2237	27	1605	2921	41	1970	3578
08	945	1733	9	1250	2282	28	1615	2939	42	2015	3659
07	975	1787									

Above table through the courtesy of the Edward Orton, Jr., Ceramics Foundation.

CHAPTER THREE

Making Ceramics

THE MAKING of a ceramic piece may be divided into six major steps:

1. Preparing the clay.
2. Forming the clay into the shape of some object.
3. Decorating.
4. Biscuit-firing. (Unfired ware is called "raw," or "green." After the first firing it is called "biscuit.")
5. Applying glaze. (In liquid form.)
6. Glaze-firing. (This fuses the glaze, hardens it and brings out its color.)

Each of these steps has its "do's" and "don'ts." If they are observed carefully, the results are bound to be good.

Preparing the Clay

The clay should be in a plastic state, easy to handle. It must be of a smooth, even consistency, not too wet and not too dry. If it is too wet, it will be mushy and cling to the fingers. To correct this, put it on a plaster bat which will withdraw some of the moisture. If the clay is too dry, it will crack and crumble. To correct, add water. Clay is just right if it comes away cleanly from the fingers as it is handled.

All clay contains air. The air must be driven out. If allowed to remain in the clay, the air will expand in the heat of firing and will cause the objects to crack or burst. To drive the air out, the clay must be "wedged."

Wedging is throwing a lump of clay forcefully about twenty times on a wedging board made of wood or plaster. This drives out the air, solidifying the clay. To test whether it is solid enough to work with, hold the lump in both hands and cut it through the middle on a taut wire. If little holes appear on the cut surfaces, throw one half of clay, cut side down on board. Throw other

half, cut side up on top of the first half. Continue to wedge. Cut clay several times to test it. When no holes appear and the texture is even and smooth, the clay is ready for use.

The warmth in the fingers dries the clay as it is being manipulated. Keep a bowl of water handy in which to dip the fingertips whenever the clay becomes slightly dry. Clay waiting to be used should be kept covered with a damp cloth.

Avoid getting clay too wet.

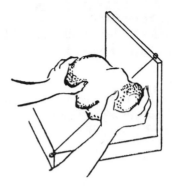

Forming with Coils

1. Wedge clay.

2. Spread oilcloth on worktable, smooth side down.

3. With both hands roll a piece of clay till it is about ½″ in diameter and 1 ft. long. It should be as uniform as possible.

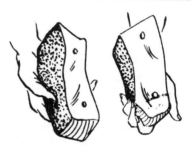

4. Twist into a disc to form the base of a bowl.

5. When disc is big enough, detach coil and gently smooth base with fingertips until surface is completely level.

6. Turn it over and smooth under surface.

7. Score (scratch with a knife)—to prepare the surface for better adhesion—the top of the outer edge of base and apply adhesion slip.

8. Put one layer of coil on the slip and attach its ends in a diagonal joint. Smooth the joint so that it is invisible.

9. Apply adhesion slip inside between wall and base and wedge a thin roll of clay into the seam to eliminate any separation.

10. Set coil a little to outside of preceding coil if shape is to go outward. Likewise, set coil a little to inside if shape is to go inward.

11. Build up as many layers of coils as needed using slip between each layer.

12. Smooth the coils inside till all spaces are solidly filled and there are no more lines.

13. Outside may or may not be smoothed. The design made by the coils is often desirable.

14. When smoothing the inside with fingers of one hand, brace outside with fingers of the other hand and vice versa. Be sure not to lose the shape of the object by too much pressure. Maintain uniform thickness throughout.

15. If clay bowl is too soft to work on, wait a little while till it becomes firmer.

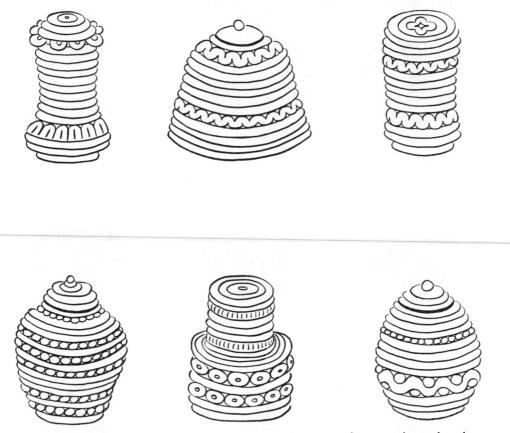

When skill with coils has been acquired, more intricate forms such as the above illustrated cookie jars and lamp bases may be attempted. The effects are achieved by twisting the coil into loops, circles, zig-zags, doughnuts, etc. It is possible to create an infinite number of combinations and designs.

The pottery pictured above are made with coils. They are smoothed inside but
retain the beauty of the coil design on the outside.

Beside each piece of coiled pottery is pictured a piece of identical shape, smoothed inside and outside and decorated in engobe, sgraffito, underglaze, or glaze designs. (See chapter on decorating.)

Making a Template

A template is a profile of the shape of a smooth piece of pottery, cut out of stiff board. It is used as a guide for uniform symmetry. It is made as follows:

1. Draw a full-size profile of the shape of the ware on a piece of board.

2. Cut out the profile as illustrated below.

3. Place pottery on a turntable or round bat and turn the ware so that the outside moves against the template. The template is held in place with one hand while the other hand does the turning. This may also be done on the pottery wheel.

Building a Head with Coils

1. Build a cylinder 3½ times as tall as its diameter out of coils 1″ thick.

2. Place cylinder on a plaster bat; smooth cylinder inside and outside.

3. Halfway down inside the cylinder, working from the top, push outward with fingers to form an oval or egg shape which is the basic form of a head.

4. Put a prop of clay under the chin to support it until the form is firm enough to hold its shape.

5. Leave top open. Retain original diameter for bottom half of cylinder. Let clay dry until

it is firm enough to hold its shape, yet soft enough to be modeled.

6. Divide front of oval into 3 equal parts horizontally. Draw a line lightly down center vertically.

7. Just below top division push in two sockets for the eyes. Inside the head the socket will appear as a round bump.

8. Place finger on the center of the bump and push outward. On the outside the effect will be the ball of an eye inside its socket.

9. For the nose, form a piece of clay into a pyramid as long as the middle third of the head.

10. Score place where nose is to be attached. Apply thick adhesion slip and attach the nose.

11. Divide bottom third into 3 equal parts horizontally.

12. One-third down, cut a horizontal slit in the clay. From inside the head, push the slit outward and the basic shape of a mouth will appear.

13. Shape contours of the head. Work from inside as much as possible.

14. Close top of head after you are satisfied with its general shape.

15. Hair, ears and shoulders are put on with additional pieces of clay. The cylinder of the neck goes down to the bottom of the form as is indicated by the dotted lines in the illustration.

16. Be careful not to make the upper part of the head too thick or the base will not be able to support the top.

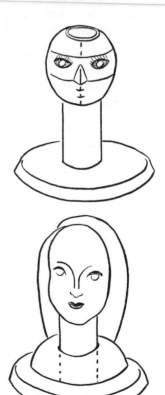

Remember, all ceramic pieces of fair size must be built hollow. When the clay being shaped is more than ¾" thick, there is danger of its cracking or breaking in the firing. It is preferable to start with coils an inch thick, and then thin the wall to ¾" in the process of modeling and refining the form.

In building any sort of a figure, be sure the hollow space inside is not hermetically sealed. There must be some opening, however tiny, to allow the air to escape during the firing.

Pinch Bowls

(This method is good for small pieces.)

1. Make a ball of wedged clay about as big as a large egg by rolling between the palms.

2. Open up ball by holding it in palm of one hand while pushing the thumb of the other hand into the center till it is ½" from the bottom.

3. Pinch ball all around with fingers of one hand while revolving clay in the palm of the other hand. Work near the bottom first, gradually coming up to the top.

4. Work for a smooth, even thickness of about ¼" all around.

5. This piece can be shaped into a variety of forms such as:

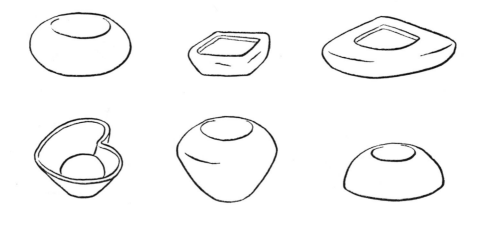

This method may also be used to combine a few pinchbowl forms and cylinders to make a composite figure as illustrated in the candlesticks below:

 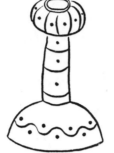  

In each of the above forms it is necessary for the cylinders to extend to the bottom level of the skirt to provide solid support. (Note illustration at extreme right.)

Slab Method

The slab method lends itself very well to the building of geometric shapes such as are shown on page 33.

Making a Covered Jar

1. Design the jar and make a paper pattern.

2. Lay 2 strips of wood ¼" thick parallel on the rough side of oilcloth, about 10" apart.

3. Wedge clay and place between the strips.

4. Roll out clay with a clean rolling pin. (Doweling stick 1" in diameter may be used instead.) Roll from center upward and downward. The strips at edge of board serve as a guide for the uniform thickness of the clay.

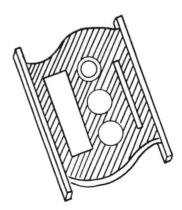

5. Place paper pattern on slab and carefully cut it into clay with a sharp, pointed tool, holding tool perpendicular to the table.

6. Remove paper pattern and all excess clay; allow cut-out pieces to become slightly firm but still pliable.

7. Wherever parts are joined, the clay should be scored (scratched with a knife) and painted with thick adhesion slip to form a more perfect bond.

8. Cut the ends of the rectangle (wall of jar) on the bias so that a diagonal joint may be made when the cylinder is formed.

9. Score the base and join it to the cylinder with adhesion slip.

10. Wedge a thin coil of clay inside between sides and base and smooth it well.

11. Turn jar upside down and attach foot by scoring and applying adhesion slip. Wedge clay into the seams.

12. Attach the ridge to the lid. The ridge serves to keep the lid from sliding off the jar. Check circumference of ridge to make sure it will fit inside the mouth of the jar.

13. Shape lid-handle from a coil of clay. When lid and handle are both leather-hard, score place of joint, and attach both pieces with adhesion slip.

14. With flexible steel scraper smooth the surfaces of the jar and lid.

15. Set aside to dry. When bone-dry, smooth and round off all sharp edges with fine sandpaper.

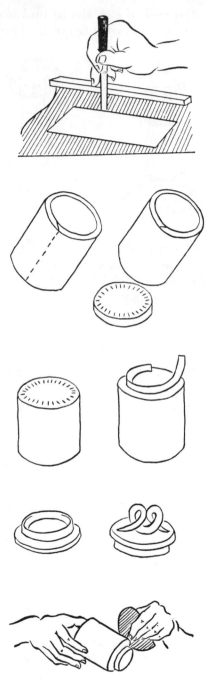

POTTERY MADE BY THE SLAB METHOD

At this stage the piece is in what is known as the "green" stage. It is now very fragile and must be handled very carefully. Never lift an unfired piece by its weak part. Always support it from underneath.

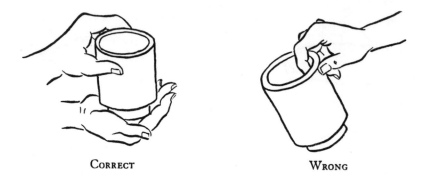

CORRECT   WRONG

Making an 8″ Plate

1. Roll out a large slab of clay on oilcloth between two parallel strips of wood about 10″ apart.

2. Cut out a 10″ disc of clay.

3. Place an 8″ pie plate bottom side up on the work table and cover it smoothly with a piece of damp cheesecloth.

4. Remove wood strips and excess clay from disc. Smooth disc with a damp sponge.

5. Place disc smooth side down over the cheesecloth covering the pie plate, in the center. It is easy to keep the clay disc intact by lifting simultaneously the disc and the oilcloth underneath it.

6. Gently shape clay to conform with shape of the pie plate. Remove oilcloth. Trim edge of plate with a knife.

7. Smooth outside of clay plate with a sponge.

8. When clay is firm enough to hold its shape, turn both plates face up. Remove metal plate by lifting it with the damp cloth under it. To prevent cracking of the clay plate, do not allow it to become too dry before separating the metal plate from it.

9. Correct all imperfections inside plate while it is still moist. Round off edges and set aside to get bone-dry.

10. Smooth with fine sandpaper.

Free Forms

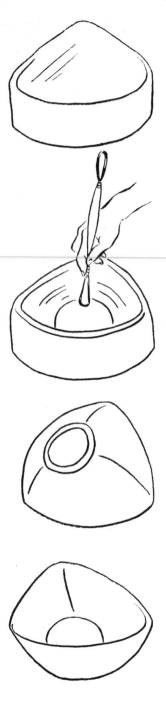

1. Shape thoroughly wedged clay into a solid geometric mass, such as a rectangle, sphere, oval, etc.

2. When clay is slightly firm, carve out the center of the mass with the wire end of a modeling tool. Carve to within ¾″ from the bottom.

3. When clay is leather-hard, turn it upside down and carve the bottom of the shape to conform harmoniously with the shape of the first carving.

4. Maintain a uniform ⅜″ thickness of wall.

5. Carve ⅜″ out of center of the bottom to form a foot.

6. All edges must be rounded. Smooth with damp sponge. When leather-hard, smooth with flexible steel scraper. Rub with fine sandpaper when bone-dry.

This method is called "free form" because it enables one to depart from the conventional to create original shapes. (See illustrations on the following page.)

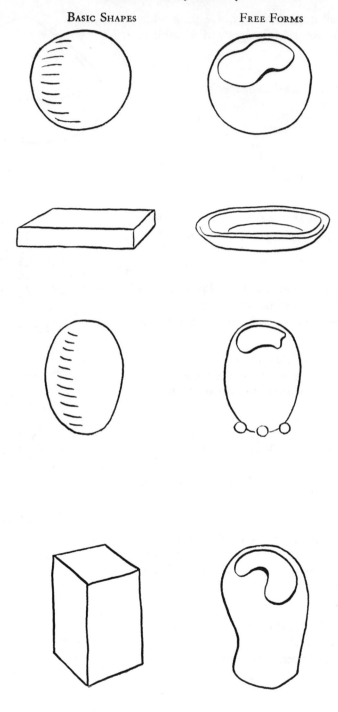

BASIC SHAPES   FREE FORMS

Modeling

The beginner should start with a simple figure, a copy of a little statue perhaps, or else something purely imaginative. Do not strive for realistic detail. The figure should have the rhythmic, rounded quality which is so characteristic of clay. To get that quality, do most of the modeling with the fingers. The more one works, the more will ideas for creation come to the mind, and the greater will be the enjoyment in handling the soft, plastic clay.

Ceramic sculpture has this great advantage over sculpture which is cast: the original on which the artist's fingers worked is preserved.

Ceramic sculpture and figurines must be hollow. The coil method, already described, is one way of making hollow pieces. Another way is to make a temporary armature, or core, and build the figure around it in such a way that the core may be removed easily without affecting the shape. If the core were left inside, the figure would crack when the clay shrinks.

Building on a Core

1. Make a rough drawing on paper of the shape and size of the figure.

2. For the core, get a piece of wood upon which to build the figure. The wood should be cone shaped. Size and thickness of the wood should depend on the size of the figure to be built. (A piece of cardboard shaped into a cone, with the seam taped up with gummed paper or scotch tape, may be used instead of wood.)

3. Wrap wood smoothly and not too tightly in a clean, damp cloth. Remove loose splinters or threads to prevent them from lodging in the clay.

4. Press bands of wedged clay all around the core. Be sure all bands are well knit together to avoid air pockets, and to form a fairly uniform thickness (about ½″) of wall.

5. Shape the large masses of figure first. Study their proportions. When they are satisfactory, put in the smaller masses. Details such as arms, ornaments, etc. are put in only after the full basic structure of the figure is reached. Always develop the figure as a whole from its crudest stage to the finish.

6. When the basic form of the figure is established, and the clay is firm but still wet, the core should be removed. If the core is allowed to remain in the figure until the clay is dry the shrinkage of the clay would grip the core and make its removal impossible without injury to the figure.

The core method is suitable for medium and large pieces.

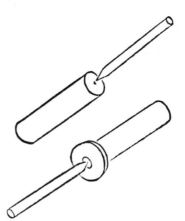

Building a Small Figurine

(*Without a Core*)

1. Make a coil of wedged clay, about 2″ in diameter.

2. Push a long pencil or ½″ pointed doweling stick through the length of the coil in the center. Twirl the stick around to widen the hole. This creates a hollow cylinder.

3. Form a disc of clay for the base.

4. Attach cylinder to base with adhesion slip and push a hole through the center of the base to connect with the hole in the cylinder.

5. Model figurine on cylinder and use extra clay for attachments such as arms, sleeves, head-dress, etc.

6. Smooth with fingers and damp sponge when **leather-hard**.

Making a Small Animal

1. Form two coils of 1½" or 2" diameter.

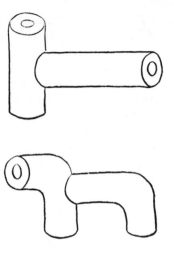

2. Hollow them out with a pencil; then join them with adhesion slip to form a "T."

3. Bend forward the top of the upright coil, and bend down the end of the horizontal one.

4. Separate the legs of the animal by cutting the lower part of both coils in half vertically.

5. The figure may or may not be mounted on a clay base. Make base or legs strong enough to support the entire figure.

6. Model the figure and smooth with a damp sponge. Set aside to dry.

Making a Doll

The china doll illustrated here was a favorite in the days of high-buttoned shoes. Now it is a collector's item. A modern version of this doll may be made as follows:

1. Build a small head using the coil method.

2. Make a semi-cylinder out of a slab of clay ¼″ thick, sloping the ends to form the shoulders. It should be proportioned to the size of the head.

3. Set the head into the semi-cylinder as illustrated. The neck must go down to the bottom level of the shoulders.

4. Make torso and limbs of cloth and stuff them like pillows. Stitch each part together at the joints.

5. Make the lower arm of a hollow cylinder so that the cloth upper arm may be inserted and glued into the hollow. Model the hand at one end of the cylinder. Make the legs and feet in a similar fashion.

6. When head and shoulders are leather-hard, carefully cut off that part of the neck which projects down into the shoulders.

7. Biscuit fire head, arms and legs. Paint features on the face with underglaze. Use underglaze also on the hair and shoes. Cover with clear transparent glaze.

8. After they have been glaze fired, apply glue to the ceramic parts wherever the body and limbs are to be inserted.

Forming on the Pottery Wheel

The pottery wheel is so ancient that references to it which predate the Old Testament are found in the hieroglyphic records of the ancient Egyptians.

Though the wheel is an aid to forming, the skillful use of the hands and fingers plays a major role; therefore, it is not considered a mechanical method of forming.

The wheel is used extensively today by craftsmen and students, and adds fascination to working with clay. It requires patience and much practice to become adept; but once the skill is mastered, there is no end to the satisfaction derived. In a few minutes it is possible to see a bowl, a dish, a plate, or perhaps a vase, of varied sizes and shapes, grow beneath the sensitive touch of one's fingers. Forming on the wheel is done in this manner:

1. Place a round plaster bat on the wheel. Anchor the bat to the wheel with soft clay. Bat should be made wet, but not to the point of saturation.

2. Throw a lump of wedged clay (about the size of a large fist) on the center of the bat. ("Throwing" is the term used by potters for forming on the wheel.)

3. Keep a bowl of water nearby. From time to time it is necessary to dip the hands into it to keep the clay in smooth working condition.

4. As the wheel revolves, press the palms of both hands around the bottom of the clay. Press it up until it is the shape of a tall cone, about 6″ high. Don't pull the clay up. Let the palms move upward as the clay rises.

5. Press down on the cone with the center of palm (while wheel is revolving), until clay is a flat, circular shape again.

6. Repeat the process of bringing the clay up and down 4 or 5 times. This conditions the clay to a fine smoothness. The Chinese potters discovered that after the tall cone is brought up, tilting it very slightly off center enables the cone to be brought down with very little pressure. This method imparts a fine working quality to the clay.

7. Now the clay mass is ready to be "opened up," *i.e.*, hollowed out. When the clay has been pressed down to a flat circular mass, place both thumbs in its center as the clay is revolving and press the thumbs downward to form a hollow.

Make hollow wider by spreading the thumbs.
Press down to within 1″ from the bottom. This
inch is allowed for a base which is to be formed
later. A cylinder has now been formed which is
the beginning of a bowl.

8. With equal pressure of the fingers of both
hands, one inside the cylinder and one outside,
bring the wall upward. (It is good practice to
make many cylinders until they can be formed
with ease.)

9. Shape the cylinder into a bowl. If the
fingers on the inside use a little more pressure
than the fingers on the outside, the wall of the
bowl will go outward, away from the center.
If the fingers on the outside exert more pressure,
the opposite will occur.

10. When bowl is fully formed, smooth it inside and out with a clean, moist sponge
while the wheel is revolving. Be sure sponge is of soft but firm texture so that no
particles will imbed themselves in the clay.

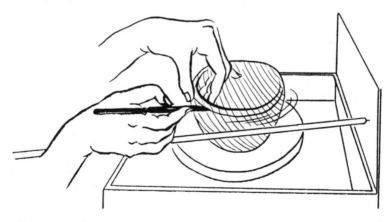

11. Level the top of revolving bowl with a knife. Steady the arm, holding the knife
against a mahl-stick for guidance. (A mahl-stick is made of 3 feet of 1″ doweling or
broomstick with a sharp nail inserted at one end.) Keep a wooden board above the
wheel level on the wall behind the wheel. Jab nail-end of the stick into the board
and hold other end in the left hand. This makes a steady prop against which the
right arm leans as it works. Some of the latest models in pottery wheels come equipped
with a rest device for steadying the arm.

12. Remove bat with bowl on it and set aside until leather-hard. The wheel is now free to be used for making another shape while the first is drying.

13. Allow bowl to dry evenly. It shrinks as it dries. If one part is permitted to dry faster than another, one part will shrink faster and cause a crack. In a bowl or vase, the rim dries fastest; therefore, put a light, damp cloth over the rim.

14. When bowl is leather-hard, place it with the bat on which it stands back on the wheel. Remove bowl from bat with a fine wire drawn tightly between both hands.

15. Turn bowl upside down and anchor it to the center of the bat with 4 lumps of clay. A good way to find the center is to hold a pencil point on the bat as it revolves. The circle drawn on the bat becomes a guide.

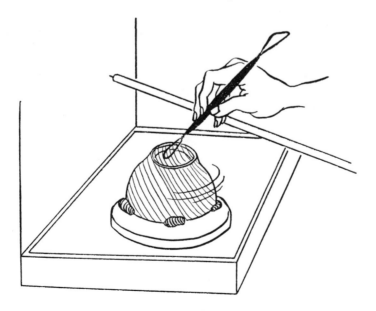

16. As the wheel revolves, refine the outside of the bowl with a turning tool. Steady the hand which holds the tool against the mahl-stick.

17. Form a foot at the bottom of the bowl by scooping out its center ¼″ to ⅜″ deep. The rim of the foot should be ¼″ to ⅜″ wide.

18. Turn bowl right side up. Anchor it in the center again with 4 lumps of clay and use a modeling or turning tool to refine the inside.

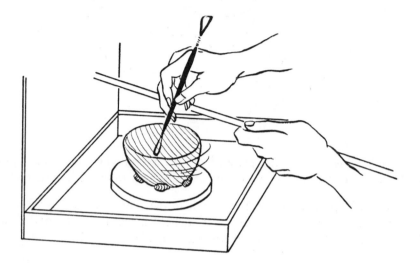

19. Smooth the revolving bowl inside and outside with a damp sponge and set it aside to dry slowly and uniformly.

Mold Making

If several copies of a certain piece are desired, make a plaster mold of it to use for casting.

Making a One-piece Mold of Illustrated Bowl

1. Build a clay model of the bowl by coil or wheel. It may be a solid mass of clay in that shape. The smoother and finer the shape, the finer the mold will be.

2. Set level on a worktable a wooden or linoleum covered board. (A marble slab or sheet of glass may also be used.)

3. Paint board with thin slip. Place model bottom side up on the board. The slip makes the model stay in place. Encircle model with a cottle (retaining wall made of a long strip of corrugated board or linoleum; this wall must be at least 3″ higher than the bowl and there must be a space of 2″ between the wall and the model).

4. With clay, seal the outside of the wall where it meets the table. Also seal the joint of the wall. This is to prevent the plaster from leaking out. The next step is mixing the plaster.

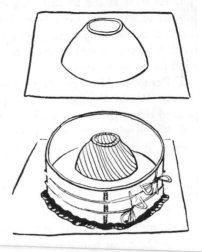

How to Mix and Pour Plaster

1. Use as much cold water as would fill the space between the wall and bowl to a level 2″ above the bowl. Pour water into a clean enamel basin or mixing bowl.

2. Sprinkle the plaster into the water scattering it over the entire surface. When plaster begins to remain on the surface of the water, enough has been used. (The usual ratio is 2½ lb. plaster to 1 qt. water.)

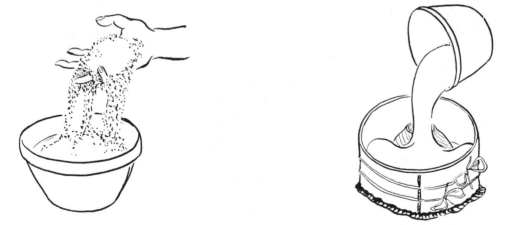

3. Let mixture stand 2 or 3 minutes; then, to break up lumps, stir slowly in one direction with the hand beneath the surface. Skim off any air bubbles that rise to the top. If air bubbles are not removed, they cause pinholes in the mold.

4. As soon as the mixture begins to thicken pour it inside the cottle, around the model, in a steady, even flow. Plaster thickens rapidly. If allowed to become too thick, it cannot be poured. The plaster must fill all the space around the model and reach a level 2″ above its top. Shake work table gently to level the plaster and bring air bubbles to the top.

5. Remove all unused plaster from mixing bowl onto a piece of newspaper immediately. Wash all utensils before plaster hardens on them. Plaster should never be poured down the drain, for it clogs the pipes.

6. When plaster begins to set it becomes warm. Since it takes several hours to harden, it is best not to move the mold until the next day.

Cleaning the Mold

1. Remove wall and turn mold upside down.

2. Remove clay model from mold with a blunt, wooden tool. Be very careful not to mar the mold which is very soft at this stage and can be nicked easily.

3. Wash mold with plain water and a soft sponge. The function of the plaster mold is to absorb moisture from the wet clay casting. The pores of plaster are sealed by soap or oily substances; therefore, never use the latter on the casting surfaces of a mold. Set aside for 2 or 3 days to dry. Never put a plaster mold on a radiator or other hot place to hasten drying. Plaster deteriorates at 120° F. and becomes unfit for casting. A well-made mold should yield about 60 good castings.

Making a Two-piece Mold

The pottery illustrated on page 48 are samples of shapes which require a two-piece mold. The nature of these forms would make their removal from a one-piece mold impossible. A demijohn, the last shape shown on page 48, is used here as a model for making a two-piece mold:

1. Make a clay model of the demijohn without the handle.

2. Divide model in half with a lightly drawn line.

3. Stuff mouth of model with a cylinder of clay about 2″ high.

4. Imbed one-half of model in a smooth, level bed of clay large enough to provide for 2″ of space all around except where it is stuffed. (See illustration.) Be sure clay bed does not reach above the half-line mark on the model.

5. Encircle bed with a wall of cardboard or linoleum (cottle) 3″ taller than the highest surface of the model. Cylinder in mouth of demijohn must touch the wall.

6. Seal all seams and openings in the wall with soft clay.

7. Pour in plaster to a level 2″ above the highest part of the model. Shake work table gently.

8. Allow at least five hours for plaster to harden. Remove wall and turn mold upside down. Remove all clay from model and mold.

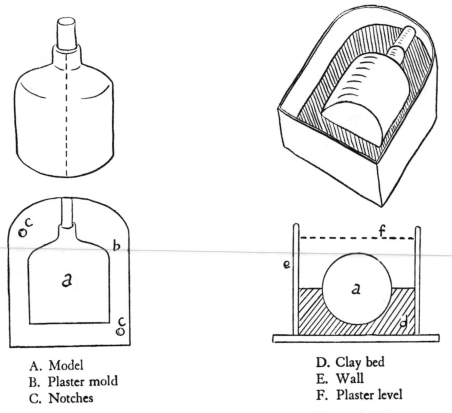

A. Model
B. Plaster mold
C. Notches

D. Clay bed
E. Wall
F. Plaster level

9. With a teaspoon scoop out one notch on each side of the mold. The purpose of the notches is to lock both sides of the mold when the pieces are joined.

10. Tie the wall around the mold and seal openings with soft clay. Paint well all plaster surfaces with separator (see page 11).

11. Pour in new plaster to a level 2″ above the highest point of the model. Shake table gently.

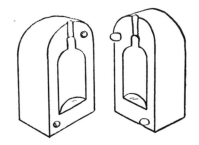

POTTERY FORMS REQUIRING TWO-PIECE MOLDS

12. Leave overnight to harden. Separate mold by prying a wooden wedge between the two halves. Tap wedge gently with a hammer.

13. Remove model carefully without injuring the mold. Use no hard tools. If model does not come out easily, run water over it.

14. Wash mold clean with sponge or brush. Use no soap. Set aside 2 or 3 days to dry.

Making a Handle

1. Draw exact shape of handle on a piece of paper.

2. Make a small coil of clay as thick as the handle should be and shape it to the drawing on the paper.

3. When demijohn and handle are both leather-hard, score places to be joined and attach handle with thick adhesion slip.

For longer handles, such as those on pitchers, tea pots, or mugs, use the "drawn" method. This is done as follows:

1. Shape a ball of wedged clay about 5" in diameter into a long pear.

2. Hold wide end of clay in one hand, and with the fingers of the other hand gently and gradually draw or pull the narrow end downward. Wet the fingers frequently to facilitate the pulling.

3. When clay is drawn to the desired length and width, detach the excess. Shape the drawn clay into a handle and attach it to the body when both are leather-hard.

To make a number of identical handles, use a press mold.

Making a Teapot

A covered bowl may be made into a teapot by adding a spout and a handle.

1. With a stick or pencil ¼" in diameter pierce

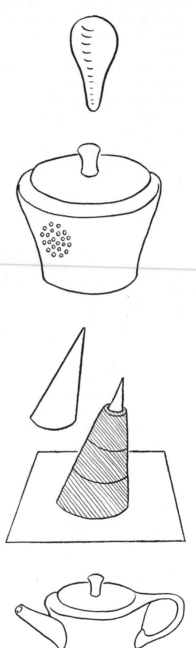

holes into the bowl where the spout is to be attached. Smooth away all rough spots with a damp sponge.

2. Build a spout with bands of clay ¼" thick over a tilted cone-shaped core made of cardboard as illustrated **on page 49.**

3. Make a drawn handle into the proper size and shape.

4. Score places of attachment and attach spout and handle with adhesion slip when all parts are leather-hard.

5. Be sure the shapes of the spout and the handle harmonize with that of the pot.

Making a Press Mold

1. Make a clay model of the handle.

2. In a cardboard box big and **deep** enough to provide 2" of space under, above, and all around the handle, put a level layer of clay 1" thick.

3. Imbed half the handle horizontally into this layer of clay.

4. Paint box with slip.

5. Pour in 2" of plaster. Allow to harden.

6. Remove from box and turn mold upside down. Remove clay bed leaving the exposed half of the handle smooth.

7. Scoop out one notch on each side of mold.

8. Set a wall around mold. Seal all openings. Paint all **surfaces** of plaster and wall (but not the **model)** thoroughly with separator.

9. Pour in 2" of plaster. Allow to harden.

10. Remove wall. Separate mold.

11. Remove model and clean mold with water and soft sponge or brush.

12. Carve a channel ¼" deep in both pieces of the mold. Follow the outline of the handle and leave a sharp ridge between the handle and the channel. Ridge should be slightly lower than the level of the outer edge of the mold.

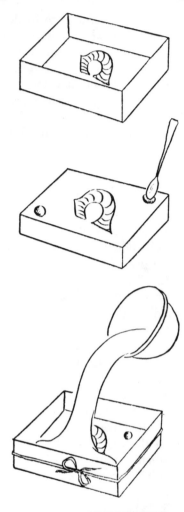

13. Avoid undercuts in any mold. An undercut is a shape which locks the clay into the mold and makes removal of the cast impossible without injury.

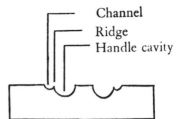

These are undercuts.

14. After mold is clean and dry, dust lightly with cornstarch. (This helps the casting to come out of the mold easily.)

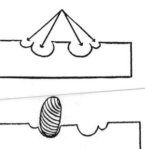

15. Put a small lump of plastic clay into the handle cavity of the mold and press both sides together. This forms the clay into a handle and the excess clay is forced into the channel.

16. Open mold to remove handle. When handle is leather-hard, clean off ridges with a knife and sponge.

The above type of press mold casts solid. Since large objects must be made hollow, this mold is good only for shapes no thicker than 1″. It can be used very nicely for small, simply carved figurines as those illustrated below:

A press mold suitable for hollow casting is made in this way:

1. Build a clay model simple enough to be cast in two pieces.

2. Follow the first eleven directions for making the mold. Avoid undercuts.

3. After mold is clean and dry, dust it lightly with cornstarch.

4. Press small pieces of clay firmly into both halves of the mold. Take care that each piece of clay is well knit into the other. The clay should be pressed about ¼" to ⅜" thick. For a very large piece, it may be ½" thick.

5. Allow about half an hour for the plaster to absorb the moisture from the clay. Cut edges on the bias all around so that when both halves of casting are attached they will form a diagonal joint.

6. Remove casting from mold. Score edges and join both halves neatly with plenty of thick adhesion slip.

7. Fill in any wrinkles or holes on the outside of the casting. Trim the seams with a knife and smooth with a damp sponge. Set aside to dry.

8. When the casting is bone-dry, obtain a final smooth finish with fine sandpaper.

Another method of pressing is to roll out slabs of clay ¼" thick, large enough to fit into both halves of the mold. Smooth slabs with damp sponge and place them inside mold, smooth side down. Press into shape of mold gently with damp sponge.

Molds may be made of many parts. The more intricate the model, the greater the number of pieces in the mold. Most important of all, avoid undercuts in designing a model for a mold.

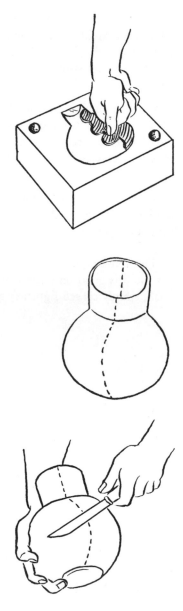

Casting

A FEW GENERAL RULES:

1. Make sure the mold is clean.

2. Mold should be slightly moist. Recognition of the proper amount of moisture comes with experience.

3. The first casting should be discarded because it absorbs the scum formed in the plaster during the process of setting.

4. Dust inside of mold lightly with cornstarch before each casting. This helps to get the cast out of the mold easily.

5. It takes approximately one half hour before a cast may be taken from the mold.

6. When the mold has absorbed much water from several castings, the cast must remain in the mold longer. Give the mold a chance to dry out properly.

7. Don't remove cast until it is firm enough to hold its shape.

8. If cast is kept in mold beyond the leather-hard state, the cast may crack.

9. Clean all seams and imperfections on the cast while it is leather-hard.

Slip Casting

A ONE-PIECE MOLD:

1. Casting slip should be smooth and creamy in consistency. Stir and put slip through a strainer before pouring.

2. After inside of mold is dusted with cornstarch, pour a steady stream of slip into the center of the mold until the slip is level with the top.

3. The slip level will sink as the mold absorbs water. Add enough slip to keep it level with the top of the mold.

4. The slip visibly forms a shell of clay inside the mold. The longer the slip remains in the mold, the thicker the shell becomes. When the shell reaches the desired thickness, pour off the excess slip.

5. Clean all clay from top of mold with a dull knife or sponge.

6. When cast becomes leather-hard, it drops out easily if mold is turned upside down.

7. Handle the cast very carefully in this fragile state and set it aside to dry.

8. Smooth with fine sandpaper when bone-dry.

A Two-piece Mold (Casting the Demijohn):

1. After both halves of mold are dusted with cornstarch, tie them together tightly. Insert wedges of wood into cord to make it tighter.

2. Seal side and bottom seams with clay.

3. Pour a steady stream of strained slip into center of mold.

4. Keep slip level with top of mold until the cast reaches desired thickness.

5. Pour off excess slip.

6. Clean all clay from top of mold.

7. Set upside down over a bowl to dry. Prop two sticks under the mold so it does not touch the bottom of the bowl.

8. Look at the mouth in about three-quarters of an hour. When clay has shrunk away from the mold completely, untie and carefully separate the two halves.

9. Remove demijohn when it is firm enough to be handled.

10. Above the mouth of the demijohn is a spare piece of clay. Remove it with a knife where it joins the mouth. Round and smooth the rim. Trim seams and fill in any holes with clay from the spare.

11. Attach the handle with thick adhesion slip at each joint. Make sure the clay in the handle is as moist as the demijohn; otherwise the handle will come off as it dries. The ideal joining stage is when both parts are leather-hard.

12. Trim seams with a knife and smooth with damp sponge.

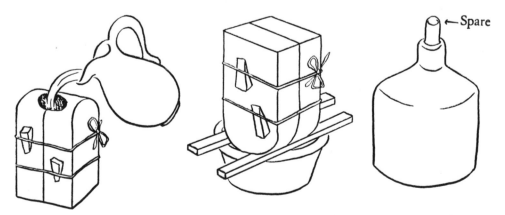

←Spare

CHAPTER FOUR

Decorating

THERE are numerous possibilities for decorative effects in ceramics. Here are given the basic techniques. When the student has mastered these, he has the means to invent, with a little creative ingenuity, a great many combinations which will yield fascinating results.

Sgraffito

1. When ware is moist leather-hard, apply a coat of colored engobe or slip contrasting to the color of the body. Use a soft, broad, flat brush. It should be so heavily laden that the slip will flow onto the body when applied. Let it flow on in one direction over an entire area. Coating must be as even as possible. Slip should be of a medium consistency. It should be well stirred before using. When first coat ceases to be shiny-wet, apply second coat in the opposite direction. Similarly, apply a third coat with brush going in first direction.

2. With a nutpick or sharp-pointed pencil, scratch a design through the engobe so that the color of the body shows through the design.

3. When piece is thoroughly dry it should be biscuit-fired.

4. Wipe biscuit-fired piece with damp, clean sponge and cover with a transparent glaze $\frac{1}{32}''$ thick. Give piece a second firing to harden and fuse the glaze. (See chapters on glazing and firing.)

Slip Painting

1. Ware should be somewhat moister than leather-hard. If body is light in color, paint design in dark colored slips. If body is dark, use light colored slips. Apply with a pointed camel's hair brush.

2. The best designs are obtained with freehand use of the brush. The student should strive to develop this skill. Some of the finest examples of free brush work can be seen in Chinese and Japanese pottery.

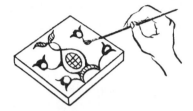

3. The novice who is too timid to paint freehand may draw the design on a piece of paper in exact size for the ware. The paper is then properly placed on the ware and the design is transferred by being pricked through lightly with a pin.

4. Slip should be well stirred. It should have a medium creamy consistency and be applied with a full brush 1/16" thick as evenly as possible. Use two coats if necessary. First coat must be somewhat dry before application of second coat. If slip is not applied properly the design will appear streaky after the glaze-firing.

5. After it is thoroughly dry, the piece is biscuit-fired. Then it is covered with a clear glaze and glaze-fired.

Slip Tracing

The slip tracer is a small rubber bulb or syringe with a nozzle. The bulb is filled with slip. The bulb is pressed gently causing a line of slip to flow as the hand moves the nozzle into a design. Slip used in a tracer should be like thick cream and well stirred. The designs should be simple, large and free. The ware should be somewhat more moist than leather-hard when slip is applied.

Encaustic or Inlaid Design

1. Ware should be leather-hard. Carve a design into it about ⅛" deep.

2. Fill in design with colored slip using a slip tracer.

3. When slip sinks into the groove, fill in more until slip is level with the rest of the surface. If, after it is dry, the slip reaches above the level of the piece, the surface may be scraped level with a knife.

4. When thoroughly dry, biscuit-fire. Use a clear glaze and glaze-fire.

Incised Line

1. Ware should be leather-hard. Scratch a line 1/16" deep to form a design. Varying widths of line may be used depending upon the design.

2. When ware is thoroughly dry, biscuit-fire it.

3. Cover it with a colored transparent majolica glaze and have it glaze-fired. The color will be darker where the glaze falls into the incised lines .

4. When ware is leather-hard, the incised lines or spaces may be filled with colored engobes or oxides instead of colored glaze. After ware is biscuit-fired, cover it with clear transparent glaze.

Various interesting and beautiful effects can be obtained by combining any or all of the above-mentioned types of decoration.

Forming Texture

The soft, plastic nature of clay invites the fingers and tools to press into it a great many designs and textures. It is fun to gather up all one's tools, such as a knife, fork, spoon, modeling tools, string, or rope, to experiment on a flatly rolled out piece of clay. See how many different textured designs can be gotten by pressing into the clay horizontally, vertically, diagonally, in circles and in combinations. This type of decoration, if used with good taste, may be applied to pottery, tiles, and figurines to good advantage. Natural shapes like leaves, grasses, twigs, bones and shells may be used in a similar way.

A rough texture may be imparted to clay by mixing it with coarse grog. Another method is to press sawdust into the surface of the ware after it has been formed and is still wet. The sawdust burns out in the firing and leaves a pitted texture.

A sparkling effect may be given to clay by mixing about 20% vermiculite (ground mica) into it. Ware made of this mixture is able to withstand more rapid cooling or heating.

Raised Modeling

1. With a rolling pin, roll out clay about $\frac{3}{16}''$ thick. Make a paper pattern of the design and place it on the clay. Cut out as many repeats of the design as required. Remove excess clay.

2. Attach designs to the ware with adhesion slip.

3. With finger tip, smoothly blend the sharp edges of the design into the ware. Use modeling tool to model and shape the design.

Sprigging

A sprig is a raised design cast in a mold and attached to the ware. This is used when many pieces of the same design are needed.

1. Build original model of the design in clay.

2. Make a plaster mold from it.

3. After dusting mold with cornstarch, press in clay.

4. Level clay with a knife.

5. Remove cast. (A piece of plastic clay pressed against the cast will help to pull it out easily.)

6. Attach cast to ware with plenty of thick adhesion slip. Sprig and ware should both be moist leather-hard. Do not remove excess slip around edges of the attached sprig until the slip is leather-hard. Then remove it with a wooden tool.

Applied Clay Design

Clay may be rolled into very thin coils and applied to the ware with thick adhesion slip to form a design. Applied designs may also be made with clay formed into flattened balls, dots, and ribbons.

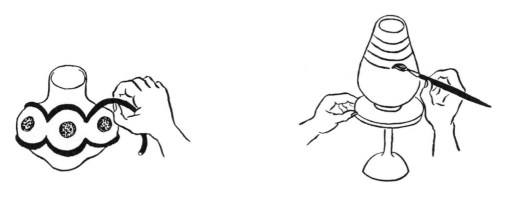

Banding

For painting horizontal bands of color on ware, place it on a turntable or potter's wheel. The wheel is revolved while a brushload of slip or underglaze is held against the ware.

Underglaze

Refractory oxides, *i.e.*, oxides which can withstand a great amount of heat (1742°–2049° F.), are used to make underglaze. It comes in powdered form in a wide variety of colors and shades, excluding orange and red. It is obtained from pottery supply companies and is used for painting designs on either raw ware or biscuit-fired ware.

Because underglaze is merely a colorant and not a glaze, the student has to mix it with a flux, i.e., a glaze material. (Order #8 Flux which is lead soda borosilicate. If that is unavailable a little clear glaze or frit [see p. 82] may be used in its place.)

Prepare underglaze in this manner:

1. Place 1 level teaspoon of underglaze on glass slab. Add 10% flux and 5% kaolin. Grind dry with a stainless steel knife or spatula.

2. Add a few drops of glycerin, a few drops of water, and 2 or 3 drops of gum tragacanth.* Grind well to a fine, smooth, creamy consistency.

The flux and the kaolin fix the color and prevent it from running on the ware. The glycerin and gum impart to the underglaze a smooth and adherent property which makes it easier to apply to the ware. Too much flux in the underglaze will cause it to run in the firing. Too little will allow the color to rub off when the piece is handled. If color is put on too thickly, or if it contains too much gum, it will peel after the firing. Apply a single coat of color with a camel's hair brush. Use a full brushload and plan the brush strokes as an integral part of the design.

Before applying the underglaze to ware that has been biscuit-fired, spray ware with a thin coat of gum tragacanth. This seals up the pores and makes easier the application of the color. The design may be drawn in pencil on the biscuit ware before underglaze is applied. The pencil marks burn out in the firing. Never erase pencil marks because erasures prevent the glaze from sticking to the ware.

After ware has been decorated with underglaze and biscuit-fired, spray (do not brush) a clear, viscous (non-running) glaze over it. The glaze should be put on between $\frac{1}{32}''$ and $\frac{1}{16}''$ thick. Application of glaze by brush would remove the color from the design.

* Recipe for gum tragacanth solution: 2 oz. gum tragacanth, 1 pt. water. Bring to a boil. Add a few drops lysol or carbolic acid to prevent formation of mould. May be stored in a covered jar. The gum comes in flake form.

Underglaze may be used on top of glazed ware before it is glaze-fired:

Apply a coat of white or light-colored opaque viscous glaze over biscuit-fired ware. When glaze is dry, spray it with a thin coat of gum tragacanth. When gum is dry, paint design on with underglaze colors. (Some potters use a bit of the white opaque glaze with the underglaze colors instead of the flux or frit.) Use a minimum of brush strokes. Design should be carefully planned because mistakes cannot be corrected in this method. This is the method employed in the decoration of Italian majolica. It was also used in the old pottery of Arabia, Assyria, and Persia.

Underglaze Pencils

Many pottery supply companies sell underglaze pencils which are made of the same materials as underglaze. The pencils are used on biscuit-fired ware only. Clear glaze is sprayed, dipped, or brushed over the design. The colors will not run. The pencils are especially good for linear designs although other special design effects also may be achieved with them.

Overglaze

A wider range of colors is obtainable in overglaze than in underglaze because overglaze matures at a lower temperature, i.e., at about cone 017–013 (1328–1517° F.).

The supply house where the overglaze is purchased usually indicates the correct firing temperature for each color. The colors are applied after the ware has been glaze-fired. Overglaze is not as durable as underglaze and in time the former will wear off. It is the chief decorative medium used in china painting. Prepare colors in this way:

1. Mix color with fat oil (a turpentine derivative which may be purchased from pottery supply companies) into a smooth, thick paste.

2. Thin with turpentine to a water color consistency.

3. Apply design on the glazed surface of the ware with a sable or camel's hair brush. All the brush strokes show; therefore plan the strokes as part of the design.

4. Set into kiln when dry and fire to proper temperature. The decoration damages easily if it is touched before firing.

CHAPTER FIVE

Tiles

In TILE-MAKING, the chief danger to avoid is warping. Any or all of the following steps will prevent this:

1. Hollow out the backs of the tiles.

2. Mix up to 20% grog into the clay as follows: Roll clay into a flat slab. Sprinkle grog over it and roll up the slab. Knead and wedge the roll thoroughly. Grog may also be added to thick slip before it is dried to a plastic state.

3. When drying tiles for biscuit-firing, separate them with little props to allow complete circulation of air. The little test tiles mentioned on page 87 are ideal for this purpose.

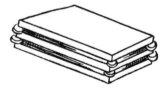

Tile-making—Slab Method

1. Roll clay flat between 2 strips of wood ½" thick. Cut clay to desired size of tile. 6" or 4" squares are generally used, though they can be made round, oval, or oblong, depending upon the purpose for which they are intended.

2. When tile is firm enough to be lifted but still damp, turn it over and hollow out 2 or 3 grooves using a wire-end modeling tool.

3. Turn hollowed side down and smooth top of tile with a clean damp sponge.

Tile Mold

To make many tiles of the same size and shape:

1. Perform step 1 of the tile-slab method.

2. Place a wall around the tile allowing 2″ space around and above it.

3. Pour in plaster to a level 2″ above the tile.

4. When plaster is completely hard remove the wall. Turn mold up and remove clay model.

This mold may be used for pressing or casting. The pressed tile casting is hollowed out with a wire-end tool, as described above. If the tile is cast, pour casting slip into the mold till it is level with the top. *When the level sinks, do not add any slip.* The tile will dry hollow.

Tile Decoration

In addition to the methods described in the chapter on decoration, tiles may also be decorated in these ways:

1. Scratch a clean incised line design into the plaster mold. This will result in a raised line on the cast or pressed tile. Colored engobes or glazes may be floated (filled in with slip tracer) into the design between the raised lines.

2. Carve a simple figure into the plaster mold. The cast or pressed tile will reproduce this figure in relief.

Tiles have many uses, some of which are wall decorations, hot-plates, table tops, trays, and name plates for the front door.

CHAPTER SIX

Jewelry

THE MAKING of ceramic jewelry holds many wonderful opportunities for originality, beauty, and variety. The student, however, should carefully avoid designs which are too fragile to be practical.

The charm and appeal of flowers are universal, but for the ceramist they present a problem; *i.e.,* how to achieve a delicate effect and yet maintain sufficient strength in the clay form. With this double aim in mind, the student must depart from realism and shape the forms in a manner suited to the material with which he is working. Petals and leaves, for instance, should be so shaped or curved as to avoid sharp, upright projections which can easily be chipped off.

Well-designed ceramic flowers are delicate, nevertheless, and when used as ornaments or jewelry, they require the same care as fine china does. Carefully handled, ceramic flower ornaments can give pleasure from one generation to the next.

Several pottery supply companies are now selling an inexpensive clay specially designed for jewelry. It fires white and reaches full maturity at cone 06, which is a desirable temperature for most students. At maturity, this clay becomes hard and durable.

Clay which is white after firing will show up the colors of the glazes more brilliantly. This does not mean, however, that many very lovely effects may not be obtained with glazes over dark clays. There is a vast field for exploration and it is up to the student to try out all sorts of combinations of clays and glazes.

How to Form Petals

1. Between the palms of the hands roll a ball of clay about ¼" in diameter. The clay should be soft and pliable, but not sticky.

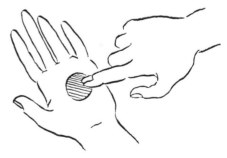

2. Place ball in center of palm of one hand. With a finger of the other hand press the ball flat. This forms a petal which takes on the

natural curve of the palm. If cracks appear when pressing, moisten the clay slightly. Thin pieces dry quickly from the warmth in the hands. Too much moisture will make the clay sticky.

The size of the petal depends on the size of the ball of clay. The shape of the petal may be varied as follows:

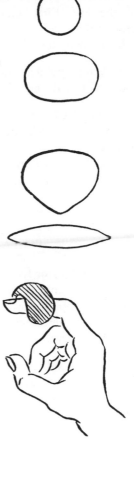

1. Round—press straight down on the ball.

2. Wide—press down on the ball and then slide the finger horizontally across the clay (while still in the palm of the hand), using pressure.

3. Taper petal at the bottom by pressing it against the palm downward.

4. Long petals, as for daisies, can be formed by rolling ball between the palms into an elongated shape, and then pressing it flat.

5. After the petal is formed, more grace may be added by curling it around the forefinger, or by pinching its outer edge between thumb and forefinger.

Leaves

1. Roll a ball of clay about ½″ in diameter between the palms of the hand. Press it at one end as it is being rolled. This will form the clay into a carrot-like shape.

2. With the finger of one hand press the carrot-shaped clay against the palm of the other hand. This will result in the shape of a leaf.

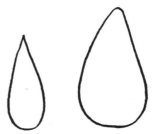

3. With a pointed tool incise the markings of the leaf. First scratch the line down the center; then add 3 or 4 branching lines to each side of the center.

4. Avoid pointed tips on leaves. Slightly rounded tips do not chip as easily.

5. Elongated leaves may be formed by rolling the ball into an elongated shape before it is pressed flat.

Here are a few of the many flowers which can be made with the petals and leaves described above:

Fruit Blossom

1. Make four or five petals. Arrange them on a plaster bat into the shape of a blossom, each petal overlapping the other slightly. Join petals by pressing the centers together with the tip of the small finger.

2. Make a ball of clay ⅜″ in diameter. Push it through a tea strainer. This creates a tassel-like little cluster. Remove it carefully from the tea strainer with the tip of a paring knife. Apply a bit of adhesion slip to the middle of the blossom and attach the cluster to it. This makes the stamen of the blossom.

A lovely pair of earrings can be made of these blossoms by cementing them to a pair of earring backs. (See chapter on sources and supplies for places where earring backs, pin backs, and cement can be obtained.)

The blossoms combined with leaves may also be used for brooches and for ornaments on various types of figurines and pottery such as ash trays, candlesticks, wall plaques, bowls, vases, and perfume bottles.

(See opposite page.)

When making a brooch, the blossoms and leaves should be attached to a foundation.

With rolling pin roll a piece of flat clay ⅛″ thick. Cut it into a rectangle about 1″ long and ¾″ wide.

In arranging the leaves and blossoms on the foundation, strive for a well-balanced design. Using adhesion slip, attach the leaves first, and then the blossoms.

Do not lift the brooch until it is firm.

The illustrated arrangement is merely one suggestion. The student eventually should try to create his own arrangements.

In order to achieve a delicate effect, use the transparent majolica type of glaze on flowers and leaves. This type comes in various colors, dark as well as light. (See chapter on glazes.)

A beautiful brooch can be made of a single large blossom or flower by using the same method as described above, but making the petals and leaves from larger balls of clay.

Roses

1. Between the palms of the hands roll a ball of clay ¼″ in diameter.

2. Press ball flat into a petal.

3. Curl up the petal in the palm of the hand. This makes the center of the rose.

4. Make 3 petals and attach them upright, overlapping and close to the curl. Gently pinch all the petals together at the bottom where they are joined.

5. Attach 4 slightly larger petals curving outward and away from the center. (Curve petals as noted on page 65, No. 5.) Petals should overlap one another.

6. When rose is leather-hard, lift it carefully and cut off the point at the bottom with a small knife. Cut as close to the flower as possible without injuring it. This creates a flat surface against which the earring back will be cemented.

The clay on the backs of earrings and pins should be scored where it will be cemented to the earring backs or pin backs. Wherever the shape permits, press the earring backs or pin-backs against the clay to make a depression into which they can be cemented. This holds them more securely. Make the depression slightly larger than the earring back or pin back to allow for shrinkage.

Rose-Necklace

1. Make 2 roses. One should be about 1¼″ in diameter; the other about 1¾″ in diameter.

2. Attach 2 small leaves to the back of the large rose.

3. A hole for stringing ribbon is made as follows: when flowers are moist leather-hard, pierce through the backs with a curved grapefruit knife. Pierce the larger rose a little above the center, the smaller one through the center. This will cause one to hang slightly lower than the other.

4. After roses are glaze-fired, string them on black grosgrain ribbon ¼″ or ⅜″ wide, through the pierced holes. The ends of the ribbon may be tied around the neck in a bow knot. A clasp attached to the ends of the ribbon can replace the bow knot.

Molded Earrings and Brooches

1. Shape a piece of clay into an oval ¼″ thick and large enough for either an earring or a brooch. Round off all sharp edges. When piece is leather-hard, carve a simple design into the oval.

2. Make a plaster mold of this model. Be sure the design faces upward before pouring the plaster.

3. Make castings by pressing clay into the mold.

4. Glaze the design in contrasting colors and textures. (See chapter on glaze.)

Other shapes, such as squares, circles, triangles, rectangles, or free forms may be used instead of the oval.

Instead of an incised design the above shapes may be ornamented with a raised design inspired by fruit, flowers, animals, sea life, people, or geometric patterns. Treat the designs conventionally or in the abstract. By cementing a pin to the back a medallion such as this can be worn as a brooch. It would also be attractive set into a metal frame.

Press pins or earring backs into the clay where they are to be cemented to form a slight hollow. Allow for shrinkage of the clay by making hollow somewhat wider than the pin or earring back.

Buttons

The cast earrings described above may be made into buttons as follows:

1. Make a shank out of a small oval of clay about ³⁄₁₆″ thick. It should be smaller than the button.

2. Make a press mold of the shank.

3. Carve a groove across the middle of the plaster mold of the button ⅛″ wide and ⅛″ deep.

4. Press clay into the mold and level the top. Lay a thick darning needle across the groove in the mold and press it down into the clay.

5. When shank and button are both leather-hard, attach them with thick adhesion slip. Keep the groove clear.

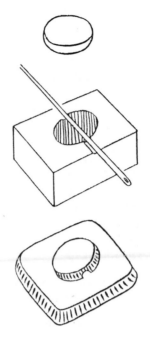

Beads

1. Roll a few coils about 8″ long. The coils may be flattened or pushed into various shapes such as illustrated.

2. When leather-hard, cut coil into beads between ¼″ to ¾″ long and pierce them smoothly with a thick darning needle. The hole should be wide enough to allow for shrinkage.

3. When beads are thoroughly dry, biscuit-fire them. They may be stacked inside a cup or bowl which is being biscuit-fired. Do not put the beads into a bowl which is being glaze-fired because the melted glaze would cause them to stick. Much care must be used in the glaze-firing of beads (see page 79).

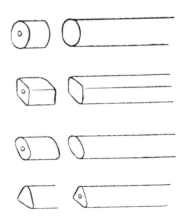

Cast Beads

Illustrated here is a bead from Perugia, Italy. It is made as follows:

1. Make a two-piece mold. Carve a groove ⅛″ wide by ⅛″ deep at each end of the plaster mold.

2. Press a metal knitting needle, ⅛″ in diameter, into the clay casting so that half the needle rests within the groove. Remove the castings and join both halves of the bead with thick slip. Trim and smooth the bead when it is leather-hard.

This bead is decorated with an underglaze design and covered with a clear glaze.

Beads and buttons may be decorated with opaque glazes of various colors and textures.

Bracelets

Two or three different sizes of beads may be combined into an interesting pattern with contrasting colors and strung on elastic thread to make a bracelet.

Button shapes may also be combined with the beads very effectively.

Many glazes are so gem-like in their colors that beautiful necklaces and bracelets can be made by combining glazed beads with pearls, coral, amber, carnelian and other semi-precious stones.

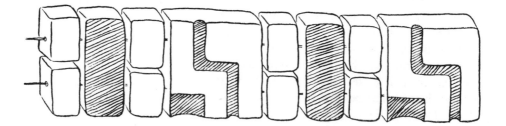

CHAPTER SEVEN

The Kiln

THE kiln is the furnace or oven in which the ware is fired. To satisfy the requirements for the types of ceramic work discussed in this book, the kiln should reach a temperature of 2000° F.

The kiln should have a peephole through which the entire fire process can be watched. A pyrometric cone is placed in the line of vision of the peephole so that the temperature of the firing can be gauged. Some kilns have temperature gauges eliminating the need for using cones. But it is advisable to have the peephole, nevertheless, so that conditions in the kiln can be observed.

Kilns are built in various sizes, from the little test kiln, 4″ x 5″ x 5″ (used for testing samples of clay and glazes, as well as for small objects such as jewelry), to the huge ones, several blocks long, which are used by large industrial plants.

Kilns may be fueled by oil, gas, or electricity.

The simplest for the beginner to operate is the electric kiln. If the kiln is to be set up in an apartment house where no more than 110 volts are available, it must be small enough to work on that voltage. (Catalogues always indicate the voltage necessary for the various models.)

It is possible to get kilns whose firing chambers are up to 11″ x 11″ x 6″, or 9″ x 9″ x 9″, which would work on 110 volts. The kiln is simply plugged in like any other household appliance. There are usually two or more switches so that the temperature may be increased slowly and gradually by turning on one switch at a time.

Choose a kiln whose heating elements are on the sides and so distributed that an even heat may be maintained throughout the firing chamber. The kiln which has its heating elements on the bottom is damaged easily by the strain of stacking and the glaze drippings.

The beginner should not attempt to fire either a gas or an oil kiln before he has had adequate instruction from one who is well experienced. The operation of such kilns requires more knowledge and care than the operation of the electric kiln because of the carbonaceous gases given off during the process of firing. These gases may be destructive to the glaze and clay if they are handled improperly.*

Oil and gas kilns are equipped with air valves which control the amount of air that is to be mixed with the fuel. The temperature increases with the amount of air in the mixture. Too little air will create a smoky, gaseous atmosphere inside the kiln. When the flame burns yellow, it is an indication that there is not sufficient air. A clear,

* Those interested in building a gas kiln may find plans in James D. Powell's excellent article published in *Science and Mechanics*, February, 1949.

purple-blue flame indicates that the mixture of air and fuel is perfect and the gases are being burnt off, thus leaving a clean atmosphere in the kiln. If too much air enters, the flame burns green, causing a waste of heat.

After gaining the necessary experience through apprenticeship, the student should know, among other things, how to burn off the gases by maintaining a proper mixture of air with the fuel, or how to use the smoky atmosphere inside the kiln to bring out fine subtleties and lustres in the glaze colors.

Because a smoky atmosphere reduces the amount of oxygen in the kiln, this is called "reduction firing." In this type of firing, the oxides used in the glazes revert to their original metallic state. Copper oxide, for instance, which in a clear flame fires green, will become red (the color of copper) in a reduction flame.

How to Build an Inexpensive Electric Kiln *

The student who would like to build a kiln for himself can do so simply and inexpensively with these materials:

46 insulating bricks
1 sheet of transite board 24" x 24"
4 single unit hot plates 660 watts each

The insulating bricks used are of the very porous, lightweight type which is easy to cut with knife or saw. Such bricks can be purchased from the Denver Fire Clay Co. or the Johns-Manville Corporation.

Transite board or a heavy asbestos board also comes from the same sources. Use a board about ½" or ⅜" thick.

Hot plate units are the simple four-legged standards used in cooking. They can be purchased in most drug or electric stores. They should be 660 watt units.

1. With a screw driver and small pliers remove from the metal table in each of the hot plates the refractory disc with the wire element in it.

2. Place the four metal tables together to form a square and drill holes in the transite board so that the tables can be attached to the board with the bolts formerly used to hold the refractory discs to the metal tables.

3. Drill small holes in transite board where the wire elements on the discs must pass through the board to connect with the cord attachments.

4. Bolt transite board to the tables with one electric cord protruding from each of the four sides.

Transite board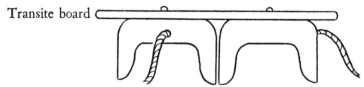

* Plan originated by Frank W. Smith.

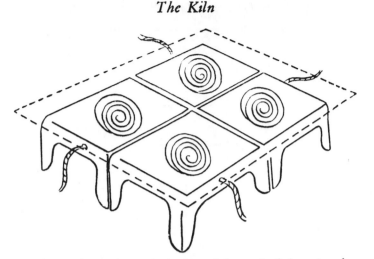

5. Untwist and straighten about six inches of the end of the wire element in each of the four discs. These discs and elements are to be set into the four inside walls of the kiln.

6. Build the four walls as illustrated below:

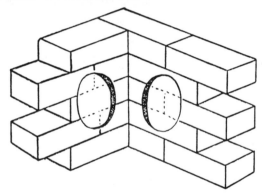

7. Place a disc on the inside center of each wall, and trace a pencil mark around the disc on the bricks.

8. Take down one wall at a time. With a sharp penknife carve into those bricks which are covered with the traced circle. Carve deep enough so that the disc can be inserted flush with the wall. Small holes should be drilled in the brick floor to permit the straightened element wires to pass down through the board and connect to the cord.

9. The kiln should now be set up exactly as it will look when finished. Lay a floor of eight bricks resting on their largest sides in the center of the transite board. If the bolts on the transite board protrude, carve little wells in the floor bricks to bring them flush to the board.

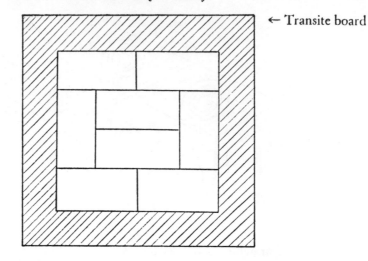

← Transite board

10. Build the walls as before and insert the discs into the circles carved out in the walls. Pass the wires down through the floor bricks to the under side of the transite board and connect the wires to the extension cords. Arrange five layers of six bricks each over the floor.

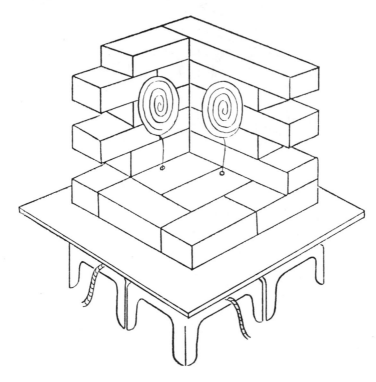

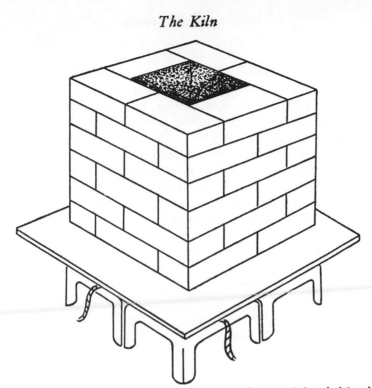

11. The top of the kiln is closed by placing the eight remaining bricks thus:

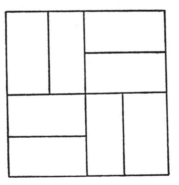

12. Drill a peephole in one of the bricks as near to the center as possible. Carve a piece of brick into a tapered plug to fit this hole.

No fastening need be used to hold the bricks together, but asbestos paper may be wrapped around the kiln walls if desired. For each firing the top of the kiln is removed and objects to be fired are stacked inside.

Best results will be obtained if each unit is switched on separately at about half hour intervals. After the kiln has been fired it should be cooled over night before any attempt is made to remove the top.

Kiln Furniture

In order to be able to fill the kiln to its maximum capacity, it is necessary to have props and shelves, which can be purchased from ceramic supply companies. They come in various sizes for convenience in stacking. They are made out of a mixture of grog and fireclay, which is a special clay that withstands very high temperatures. If the shelves and props did not have that resistance, they would sag or warp under the weight of the stacked ware in the process of firing.

Ceramic supply companies also sell a variety of sizes of stilts and triangles which are used for propping glazed ware so that it does not touch the floor of the kiln or the shelves on which the ware may be stacked. For propping very small glazed pieces such as earrings, small, flat pieces of clay are convenient.

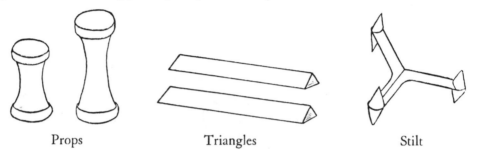

Props   Triangles   Stilt

The floor of the kiln as well as the shelves should be painted with a coat of kiln wash to protect them from glaze drippings which are apt to occur during a glaze-firing. The kiln wash is made of equal parts of kaolin and flint. Mix enough water with the latter to make a thin creamy liquid. Apply an even coating with a wide, inexpensive brush.

When glaze drippings occur on kiln floor or shelves, the drippings should be chipped off with a chisel. If they don't come off easily, sprinkle flint over them. In the next firing the flint will be absorbed into the glaze. The drippings will then yield more easily.

Stacking

BISCUIT-WARE:

In stacking ware for biscuit-firing, the pieces may touch one another, and a small, light piece may be set inside a larger, heavier piece provided no strain occurs at any point.

Tiles must be set horizontally in the kiln to prevent warping. One tile may be placed on top of another, but in order to provide for complete

Stacked for biscuit fire.

air and heat circulation, place little props between them. Little glaze test tiles may be used as props. (See p. 87.)

Plates also must be set in the kiln horizontally. They, too, may be stacked one inside the other, heaviest ones on the bottom. Some coarse grog should be sprinkled between plates to provide for air and heat circulation.

It is wise to accumulate enough ware to fill the kiln so that the most efficient use may be made of the chamber space. Allowing any of the ware to set too close to the flame or heating elements, might damage both ware and elements.

Stacked for glaze fire.

GLAZED WARE:

Stack each piece so that it does not touch any other. Leave at least ¼" space around every object in the kiln. To conserve space, try to fit the shapes of the ware; for instance, a piece that is wide at the bottom and narrow on top may be placed next to a piece that is narrow on bottom and wide on top.

Glazed beads should be strung on a wire which is able to withstand a very high temperature. High-tempered steel or nichrome wire is good for this purpose. Stretch the wire across two props in the kiln. To prevent the beads from sticking, string them on the wire without touching one to another. Allow no glaze inside the holes or at the openings of the holes.

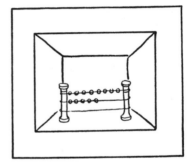

Beads stacked for glaze fire.

Firing

Clay should be heated slowly. Ware must be bathed and saturated in a gradually increasing temperature. If this process is carried on too quickly, the clay will crack or burst.

Thick pieces of clay ware require even slower and more gradual firing than thin pieces. The amount of time for the complete firing depends upon the size of the firing chamber, the size of the pieces being fired, and the temperature required to mature the ware. Since these conditions are relative, it is difficult to set down a definite rule for the time of firing. I have successfully fired a gas kiln with a firing chamber of about one-and-a-half cubic feet to cone 06, between 6 and 9 hours, depending upon how heavily the ware was stacked. I have also successfully fired an electric kiln with a firing chamber of 5½″ x 6″ x 6″ to cone 06 in two hours. These experiences are suggested to give the student a general idea of the over-all timing.

It is very important for the student to know what happens to the ware inside the kiln while the firing is going on.

Even though the ware is bone-dry to the touch and sight, the clay still contains what is called "mechanical water." This water is driven off in the first stage of firing. The firing during this period must be done so slowly that in some cases the kiln door is left open for the first hour or two. In the small electric kiln the peephole may be left open for about half an hour. The steaming vapors are visible as they escape. This is called the "water-smoking" period. Its climax is reached at about 400° F. Doors or peepholes should then be shut and a gradual adjustment for more heat should be made.

In the second stage, heating up and dehydration of the ware occur. Everything inside the kiln becomes dull red and shrinkage begins to take place.

The third stage, the period of oxidation, starts at about 1200° F. By then everything in the kiln is a bright, flaming red and the oxygen is combining with carbon, sulphur, iron, and other minerals in the clay.

The final stage is vitrification. This stage must have a wide range of temperature. It begins at about 1600° F. and continues till the desired maturity. In this stage, the glazes on the glazed ware begin to melt and glisten, while all the component particles in the clay are becoming fused or united into a new substance which is both strong and dense. The higher the fire, the more glasslike becomes the clay. But when over-vitrification is reached, the clay becomes a melted mass and the glazes burn out.

When the cone indicates the completion of the firing, the current or fuel is shut off and all openings or air valves are closed so that no draft can hit the white-hot ware.

The kiln must not be opened or tampered with until it is completely cooled off—to the extent that the ware may be handled comfortably with the bare hands. Forced or rapid cooling cracks and breaks the ware. It is also injurious to the kiln.

It is generally better to fire an all-biscuit or all-glaze kiln; but it is possible to fire a combination of biscuit and glazed ware successfully in the same kiln if both are stacked carefully and both mature at the same temperature. Set the biscuit ware in the hottest part of the kiln (generally nearest the heating units).

Ware which has been biscuit-fired should be kept in a clean closet until glaze is applied, because dust, dirt, and grease are detrimental to glazes. Too much handling of biscuit-ware may cause the natural oils in the skin to create flaws in the subsequent glazing.

CHAPTER EIGHT

Glaze

THE subject of glazing is both complicated and technical. In accord with the purposes of this book there will be used a simplified approach which nevertheless provides wide latitude for creative experimentation. After the student has become thoroughly acquainted with this treatment, he may acquire additional knowledge from the books recommended in the bibliography.

Glaze is a combination of finely ground (powdered) materials which, submitted to a maturing temperature, will fuse together and form a glassy surface.

The maturing temperature varies according to the materials of which the glaze is composed.

Glaze, like clay, shrinks in the firing. Therefore, the glaze composition must be designed to "fit" the clay body. In other words, glaze must have the same rate of shrinkage at maturing temperature as the clay to which it is applied.

A good glaze should serve the following purposes:

1. Strengthen the ware.
2. Make porous ware more waterproof.
3. Beautify the ware.
4. Make the ware (particularly when designed for dining purposes) more sanitary and easier to clean.

There are lead glazes and alkaline glazes. Lead glazes fire shiny, strong and hard. Alkaline glazes are soft in texture, porous, and can produce certain beautiful colors which cannot be obtained in the lead glazes. The alkaline glazes are well suited to art wares which do not have to be weather- or water-proof. The lovely turquoise and blues of ancient Persian and Egyptian ceramics were obtained through the use of alkaline glaze.

In former times, the potter had to grind and prepare all materials himself—a very laborious process. Today, ceramic supply companies sell glazes which are completely prepared in powder form, ready for application when mixed with water. There are many fine commercially prepared glazes obtainable in a wide variety of beautiful colors and textures. The companies usually classify such glazes as follows:

1. Majolicas—These may be transparent—or opaque. They fire to a high gloss. Because they have a low viscosity (flow freely) they can cover up any thin spots which may occur in the application of the glaze.

2. Enamels—May be translucent or opaque. They have a medium viscosity and are glossy.

3. Matt—Opaque; produce a smooth matt texture. These are viscous.

4. Antique or Art Glazes—These are mixtures of various colors and textures to produce interesting split color and mottled effects.

It is wise to order clay and glaze from the same company, to mature at the same temperature. The beginner will find that 1 lb. of glaze of any color will go a long way. Use of these prepared glazes is a great time-saver.

Many students, however, prefer to mix their own glazes to obtain a more intimate grasp of the materials and handling. They are also able to enjoy a wider latitude in getting unusual and artistic effects.

For people who want to mix their own glazes, the ceramic supply companies offer an aid in the form of prepared frits. Frit is a mixture of soluble and insoluble glaze materials which have been calcined, *i. e.*, heated to melting point, plunged into water, and then finely ground. The purpose of fritting is to change the soluble materials into insoluble form. It also reduces the maturing temperature of the glaze. Frits are made for alkaline glazes as well as for lead glazes. By itself, frit is similar to finely ground glass. It may be used by itself or in conjunction with other glaze materials, or other frits, depending upon the effect desired. When ordering frit, one should specify that it be ground to about 200 mesh.

The following basic formulas contain frits manufactured and sold by the Pemco Corporation of Baltimore, Md. They fire to cones 06–04.

#1

Frit Pb-63	92%
Kaolin	8
	100%

Add 5% raw borax and .25% magnesium carbonate. This helps to keep the glaze mixture in suspension thus giving it better working properties. The above formula makes a very stable lead compound and an excellent base for colors. When used alone and applied heavily, it produces a slight milkiness.

#2

Frit Pb-742	92%
Kaolin	8
	100%

Add raw borax and magnesium as above. This is also a lead compound and is very similar to the first glaze, but is recommended where a perfectly clear transparent glaze is desired, especially over slip painting and underglaze designs.

#3

Frit Pb-63	72%
Frit Pb-83	20
Kaolin	8
	100%

Add raw borax and magnesium as above. Pb-83 frit contains a much higher percentage of lead and, therefore, produces a glaze with a lower maturing point and a low viscosity at cones 06–04.

#4

Frit P-54	61.3%
Kaolin	8.2
Zircopax	10.2
Zinc Zirconium Silicate	20.4
Borax	1.0
	101.1%

This is an alkaline matt opaque glaze which fires at cone 04. It will produce beautiful blues when mixed with copper.

Following are formulas using frits made by the Ferro Enamel Corporation of Cleveland, Ohio:

#5		#6	
Frit 3481	90%	Frit 3403	90%
Kaolin	10	Kaolin	10
	100%		100%

Frit 3403 is a brilliant, very high lead-content glaze, but has a creamier color than frit 3481.

#7

Frit 3195	95%
Kaolin	5
	100%

This is an alkaline glaze which is transparent and glossy.

The addition of 1 or 2% bentonite to any of the glazes will keep them in suspension. A little gum tragacanth mixed into a lead glaze will counteract its tendency to rub off easily when applied.

Glaze Characteristics

A glaze may:

be clear or colored;	fire to a very glossy surface;
be transparent or opaque;	fire to a semi-matt surface;
have little viscosity in the firing;	fire to a dull matt surface;
be very viscous throughout firing;	fire to a mottled texture.

How to Adjust Glazes

Any of the above characteristics may be achieved or eliminated in accordance with the effect desired. If the student is willing to experiment a little, he will find it not too difficult to control the characteristics of his glaze.

A flowing glaze can be made stationary by adding a small amount (up to 5%) of china clay or ball clay. If 25% is added, the glaze will turn from a glossy, flowing texture to a fixed matt texture. In adding between 5% and 25%, the glaze can be made into varying degrees of glossiness, semi-matt to dull matt.

A viscous glaze may be made to flow by increasing the frit.

A mottled effect may be obtained by adding 3% black iron oxide or 3% ilmenite. In some glazes, the addition of rutile will give a mottled or matt surface.

A clear (colorless), transparent glaze may be made opaque white by the addition of 10% to 20% tin oxide, zircopax, zinc oxide, or opax.

Clear transparent glaze and opaque white glaze are considered basic for the purpose of color. When the transparent glaze is mixed with any colorants such as those mentioned below, corresponding colored transparent glazes will result. The clay body or any design on the body is revealed through these glazes. When the opaque white glaze is mixed with any of the colorants, corresponding colored opaque glazes will result. The characteristics of the colored glazes are usually the same as those of the basic glaze from which they were mixed.

Characteristics of Colorants

Antimony Oxide: Use up to 6%. Too much causes blistering. Produces yellow glaze when mixed with lead or iron. Has a tendency to opacify the glaze.

Copper may be used in the form of: black copper oxide; red copper oxide; copper carbonate. (The oxides are stronger coloring agents than the carbonates.)

In a lead glaze copper produces varying shades of green. In an alkaline glaze it produces blue greens or turquoise. 2% to 5% mixed into the glaze will vary the shades from light to dark. A larger amount will give a metallic quality to the glaze and produce a matt texture. A beautiful gun metal glaze is obtained by mixing 6% copper and 3% manganese black oxide into the glaze. Copper is a very active flux. It should be used in glazes which fire from cones 015 to 04. It changes to red in a reduction firing.

Cobalt may be used in the form of: black cobalt oxide; cobalt carbonate. This is a strong flux, highly potent in the blue it produces. Use up to 4%, which is sufficient to produce a dark navy blue. It can withstand very high temperature.

Chrome may be used in the form of: chromium oxide; potassium nichromate; lead chromate.

It does not flux easily. Glazes containing chrome should be fired at slightly higher temperatures than normal to reach maturity. Chrome should not be combined with a zinc-bearing glaze because that produces a dirty color. Combined with a large percentage of iron, chrome produces black. It is best used on a white clay body. 2% to 5% may be used. Gives a blue green in an alkaline glaze, a bright yellow green in a glaze containing borax, and pink in a glaze containing tin oxide.

Iron may be used in the form of: red iron oxide; black iron oxide; red clays (these are rich in iron oxide); ochres, siennas, and umbers.

From 1% to 5% produces amber yellows. From 5% to 10% brings the color up to a deep red-brown. In an opaque glaze it produces yellow with brown flecks. Though it is a weak flux, it has no effect on the maturing temperature. It is not affected by any temperature range.

Iron Chromate: Use from 1% to 4%. Gives beautiful effects in frit glazes. Colors are grays or browns.

Manganese may be used in the form of: manganese dioxide; manganese black oxide; manganese carbonate.

1% to 2% in an opaque glaze will give pink. May be used up to 8%, which shades into wines and purples in an alkaline glaze. In a lead glaze it produces light to dark browns. When used with cobalt or iron it will give a deep black.

Nickel may be used in the form of: black nickel oxide; green oxide of nickel; nickel carbonate.

Up to 3% may be used. It does not flux easily and withstands very high temperatures. It gives yellow-green in an alkaline glaze and bronze-green in a lead glaze. In an opaque lead glaze it produces browns, blues, or purples.

Rutile: Use from 5% to 10%. It gives a texture as well as color to a glaze. The colors it produces are ivory, tans, browns, greens, and blues, depending upon the amount used and the composition of the basic glaze.

Titanium Oxide: Use up to 10%. Produces ivory to yellow when mixed with varying amounts of iron. Has a tendency to opacify.

Uranium Oxide may be used in the form of: sodium uranium oxide, known as commercial uranium oxide; black uranium oxide.

Use from 5% to 8%. Too much causes black specks. Does not affect the maturing point of the glaze. Has a very wide range of temperature, cone 010 to 12. Produces various shades of oranges and yellows.

Various intermediate and blended shades of color can be obtained by mixing small amounts of two or three different oxides.

How to Mix Glazes

Glaze materials are measured by dry weight. A gram scale with removable metal trays is best for this purpose. Such a scale comes equipped with a set of gram weights, 50, 20, 10, 5, 2 and 1 gr. On the front of the scale is a horizontal metal rod with a sliding weight on it. The rod is calibrated for tenths of a gram.

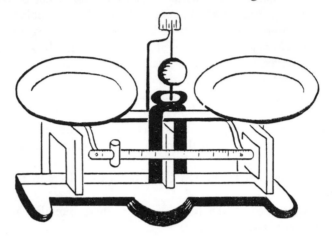

Herewith are instructions for mixing a glaze, using formula #4 on page 83 as an example:

Frit P-54	61.3%
Kaolin	8.2
Zircopax	10.2
Zinc Zirconium Silicate	20.4
Borax	1.0
	101.1%

Glaze materials must be weighed very precisely. To insure accuracy, do as follows:

Place on the table 5 sheets of paper, one for each ingredient in the glaze. Mark the name of the ingredient on each sheet. Make sure the scale is equally balanced. On the tray to the left place one 50 gram weight, one 10 gram weight and one 1 gram weight. This makes 61 grams. On the metal rod, slide the weight to the right 3/10 of a gram. Using a spoon, put enough frit P-54 into the tray on the right to balance the weights on the tray to the left. When 61.3 grams of frit have been accurately weighed, empty the tray onto the paper marked "frit P-54." Use a wide, dry brush to get all the particles off the tray. Follow the same procedure with all the other ingredients until each has been weighed and placed upon its respective sheet of paper.

Put all ingredients into the 32 oz. mortar and grind them thoroughly in dry state at least one half hour. Store the dry glaze batch in a covered jar, labeled to identify the glaze. If a larger basic glaze batch is desired, the formula may be doubled or tripled. A variety of colored glazes can be made from this basic glaze by adding colorants.

How to Color Glaze

Weigh the percentage of oxide to be put into a given amount of basic glaze. For example, if 3% of copper is to be added to 30 grams of basic glaze, the weight of the copper should be $\frac{9}{10}$ of a gram. Place oxide into the 10 oz. mortar. Add a little of the basic glaze and enough water to make a thick paste. Grind thoroughly. Add the rest of the basic glaze and grind well till the oxide is evenly permeated throughout the glaze. Add enough water to produce a creamy consistency. Put through the 80 mesh screen to break up lumps. Store in a covered jar, labeled to indicate the basic glaze, the oxide and its percentage, as well as the cone at which the glaze matures

How to Make Test Tiles for Glazes

Before using a new glaze on any ware, it is wise to test it to see its nature and its color. For this purpose, test tiles may be made as follows:

1. With rolling pin roll out a flat piece of clay ¼" thick. With a circular cookie cutter or with the cover of a small jar, cut out 12 pieces. They should be about 1½" in diameter. Smooth all edges.

2. Paint the inside bottom of a cardboard shoe box with slip.

3. Place the clay discs flat inside the slip-painted box allowing at least 1" space all around each of them.

4. Mix plaster and pour enough to rise level 1½" above the clay discs.

5. Allow several hours for plaster to set. Remove the discs from the mold and clean it with a soft, damp sponge.

By pressing clay into this mold, 12 uniform test tiles can be made in very little time. Pierce a hole through each tile while clay is leather-hard. The tiles should be biscuit-fired before they are used to test glazes. The glaze is applied on one side of the tile. On the other side is marked the identification of the glaze. A different num ber or letter may be used as a symbol for marking each glaze. Underglaze applied with a brush, or an underglaze pencil may be used to mark the tiles. The hole is for a string to attach the sample tile to the jar of the glaze.

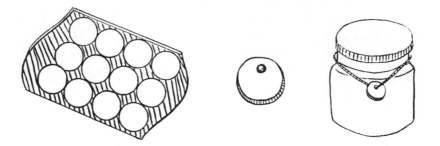

How to Apply Glaze

Ware should be handled with clean hands and cleaned with a damp sponge before glaze is applied.

If ware is very porous, thin the glaze to a light creamy consistency by adding a little water. Apply two or three thin coats. If porous ware is dampened slightly, the glaze can be applied and will adhere more smoothly. If the glaze thickens and cracks as it is applied, it needs more water. If there is too much water in the glaze, after allowing it to settle, pour off the water which remains on top. The rubber bulb used as a slip tracer serves well for removing this water.

If the ware is dense with only a slight porosity, the glaze should be of a medium creamy consistency. Large, heavy pieces should be immersed in water for a minute just before glaze is applied.

If ware is hard and has no porosity, warm it up before applying glaze which, in this case, should be thick. The heated ware absorbs the water from the glaze as the latter forms a coat on its surface.

If the glaze has a low viscosity, it should be applied about $\frac{1}{32}''$ thick. On a vertical form, such as a vase, the glaze application should be thinner toward the bottom to allow for the flow of glaze from the top. Too thick an application at the bottom will cause pools of glaze to flow off the ware.

If the glaze is semi-matt or matt, it should be applied more heavily. Two or three medium coats are better than one thick one. These coats should be applied very evenly as any thin parts will show up after the firing.

The methods for applying glaze are:

Brushing:

Use a wide brush with soft bristles. Brush must be heavily laden so that the glaze flows on to the ware in a smooth, even stream. After the first coat dries, apply the next in the opposite direction. It is generally desirable to glaze the inside of a vessel before the outside.

Pouring:

Pour glaze into the ware (bowl, vase, or cup, etc.) and twirl it around so that the inside is completely covered with an even coat of glaze. Then pour off the excess. The twirling must be done very quickly because the longer the glaze remains in the ware, the thicker becomes the coat being formed. Lay 2 flat sticks or a wire rack over a bowl or basin. Place ware upside down on the sticks or rack. Quickly pour glaze over the center of the ware so that the glaze flows evenly all over the outside. Use a knife and small, damp sponge to scrape and clean away the glaze from the foot of the ware. Unglazed spots may be touched up with a brush. Double layers of glaze may be carefully scraped to the desired thickness with a knife. The unused glaze in the basin may be put back into the original container to be reused.

Dipping:

Pour glaze into an enamel bowl or basin. Holding ware at an angle, dip it into the glaze, turning it quickly so that as much of the ware as possible is covered with glaze. Guard against getting too thick a coat. Touch up unglazed parts with a brush.

Spraying:

In spraying, much of the glaze is wasted. But this method is particularly good to use when putting transparent glazes over an under-glaze design. In large potteries the spraying is

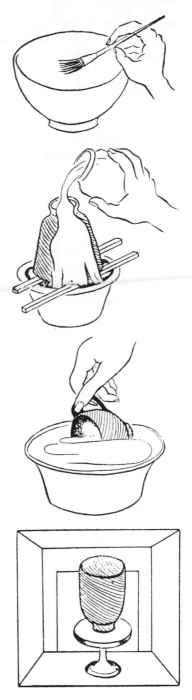

done in a booth equipped with an electric spray gun and an exhaust fan which carries off the waste, thus protecting the operator's lungs. Such equipment is expensive, but it can be improvised in the studio in this manner: place a corrugated or wooden box against an open window. Cut out an opening in the back of the box, which is next to the window. Put a turntable into the center of the box and set the ware on top of the turntable. A hand spray-gun (flit-gun) or the sprayer from an electric vacuum cleaner may be used. Thin the glaze somewhat and fill the sprayer with it. (Thick glaze will have difficulty getting through the narrow tube in the sprayer.) A mask should be worn over nose and mouth for protection. A mask may be improvised with a large handkerchief, or it may be purchased inexpensively from most ceramic supply companies.

Spray the inside of ware first, turning the turntable during the spraying to get an even coat all around. When the glaze appears wet on the ware, stop spraying and wait until it is dry. Apply the next coat only after the previous coat is dry. Spraying glaze over wet glaze merely displaces the first coat and causes it to drip.

After inside of ware is properly coated, turn it upside down and spray the outside in a similar manner. Remove glaze from foot. Set ware right side up and touch up the rim with some glaze on a brush.

Glaze Defects

After firing, where there is perfect adjustment between glaze and body, the under-surface of the glaze has penetrated and knit together with the outer surface of the body. Where this does not occur, there are defects in the glaze. The most common of these are:

Scaling or Peeling. If glaze does not shrink as much as the body, it will peel. To correct, decrease the amount of flint in the glaze or body.

Crazing. If glaze shrinks more than the body, it will craze, or form a network of fine cracks. This is undesirable in ware which must be sanitary and waterproof. To correct this, add more flint or boric acid to body or to the glaze. Crazing, however, may be used decoratively on artware to give the effect of an over-all crackle. This is done by mixing a little burnt sienna oil paint with some benzine or turpentine, applying the mixture all over the glazed surface, and then washing the piece thoroughly with soap and water. The color sinks into the fine cracks and darkens them. This should be done as soon as the ware is taken out of the kiln. The ware should not be handled more than necessary because the natural oils in the skin seal up the cracks and prevent the color from penetrating.

Blistering may be caused by the glaze not being fired to maturity, or by the presence of sulphur in the body or glaze. To correct the latter, add about 1% of barium carbonate to the clay. It may also occur when too much manganese is used.

Pinholes may be caused by too rapid firing or cooling, by dust or dirt particles on the ware before glazing, or, in cast ware, it may be caused by air in the clay body.

Dull, Faded Colors may be caused by overfiring.

Bare Spots. Oil or grease on the biscuit-ware will prevent adhesion of glaze.

Crawling. A glaze has crawled when it appears rolled up in bead-like formations leaving parts of the body unglazed. This may occur for these reasons: the unfired glaze on the ware is cracked, the biscuit-ware is underfired, or there is too much kaolin in the glaze.

Some General Facts About Glazes

Always stir glaze before using.

Sometimes the colored glaze of some ware may affect the glaze on other ware placed near it during the firing.

Many glaze defects may be corrected by reglazing and refiring. Glaze applied on fired glazed ware should be thick. If the ware is highly vitrified, it should be warmed up before the new glaze is applied.

The addition of 5% to 25% orthoclase feldspar to a glaze raises the melting point, helps to eliminate crazing, increases viscosity, and produces a matt finish.

Addition of 10% to 30% flint raises the melting point of a glaze. It also produces a matt finish and eliminates crazing.

Addition of whiting from 5% to 20% in a glaze raises the melting point and produces a matt.

When measuring and mixing glaze, care should be taken that a minimum of particles be raised in the air. It is injurious to inhale them. No harm results from dipping the hands into glaze, provided there are no open cuts or sores on the skin.

Dirt or grease on biscuit-fired ware may be burnt out by putting the ware through a firing. Glaze may then be applied to it.

When a matt glaze is overfired or cooled too rapidly, it turns glossy.

A thin piece of ware, after glaze has been applied to the inside, may be too wet to take any glaze on the outside. The outside should be glazed after the inside is dry.

When glazing sculpture, scrape off excess glaze in places where it may obscure the modeling (eyes, nostrils, hair, mouth, etc.).

A viscous glaze may be painted or traced into a design over another viscous glaze. For instance, a design in a white viscous glaze may be placed over a background of a dark viscous glaze.

A notebook should be kept on all glaze formulas and all experiments should be recorded for future reference. All jars should be accurately labeled with their contents. Glaze will not cover up or fill in cracks which occur in biscuit-ware.

Waterproofing

Glazed ware fired up to about 2000° F. may be somewhat porous. Such ware may be waterproofed as follows:

Melt paraffin in a large metal container and add 25% turpentine. Keep mixture hot and soak ware in it for about ten minutes. Remove ware and wash off excess paraffin from the surface with soap and warm water.

CHAPTER NINE

Design

In 1817, the English poet, John Keats, wrote, "A thing of beauty is a joy forever." So it is today and so it will be a thousand years from today. The delicate beauty of a Chinese vase made in the Sung Dynasty in 1000 A.D. gives joy to the beholder now just as it did to its creator in the dim past.

This is also true of the products of the modern craftsman. If he makes a thing which possesses true beauty, it will be timeless.

The first requisite of beauty in design is the integrity of its maker. A good craftsman gives the very best of his hand, heart, and mind to the object he is making. He will strive for the finest quality in the basic shape of his ware before any decoration is put upon it. He will not use embellishments to conceal bad form.

The approach to good design varies because every person expresses his own individuality through his creations. (It must be explained here that the word "design" refers to the complete composition of shape, line, color, and texture, whether it be pottery or sculpture.) There are certain universal principles, however, which are basic for all good design. They are universal because they apply to any and all the arts, and even to life itself. Design should have:

Function

In designing any ceramic piece one must bear in mind its intended use. If it is for decorative purposes, such as figures, the clay may be porous and it may or may not be glazed. Vases or bowls expected to hold water should be made of clay which is fired to maturity to insure maximum density. They should be glazed inside and out to help make them waterproof. A fruit or nut bowl should be glazed on the inside and may be left unglazed on the outside, especially if the clay has an interesting texture or color. Pottery intended to hold food should lack raised or carved designs on the inside so that they would be easy to clean. The weight of the piece should be suited to its purpose. A bird bath, for instance, should be of larger, heavier construction than a cereal bowl. The rough textured clays are more suitable for strong, rugged or peasant designs than for delicate ware.

Structure

If the piece is structurally logical and sound, its proportions will be right. Common sense is a good guide. A tiny base could not be expected to support a massive form,

93

nor is a large, heavy base necessary for a small, delicate figure. Wherever hands, feet, handles, covers, spouts, or other parts are added to the basic form, these parts should be shaped to harmonize with the form. Each part must appear necessary to the whole, and all must look as though they "belong" together.

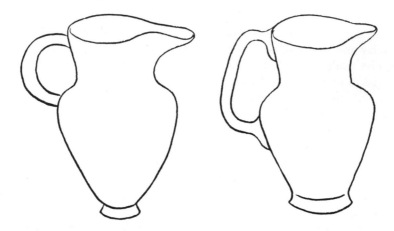

In the above illustration the pitcher on the left has a base which is too small to support the body. The lip is too large and makes the pitcher look topheavy. Pouring from it would be difficult. The handle seems stuck on without regard to its relationship to the shape of the pitcher. Also, the handle is too small in proportion to the rest of the shape. Lifting this pitcher by such a handle would be most impractical.

The pitcher to the right has the same basic shape as the one to the left, but its structure is better. The broader base gives the form a more solid appearance, and the handle appears as if it grew out of the pitcher naturally, like a branch on a tree. This handle can be grasped comfortably and is large enough to support the full weight of the pitcher. The smaller lip is more in keeping with the proportion of the entire form.

Balance

The shape of any piece of ceramics is composed of a combination of related masses. These masses impart a feeling of weight. Some look heavier than others, depending upon their size and color intensity. Often there are open shapes as well as solid ones in the composition. The mouth of a vase, the hole created by a handle, the spaces between arms and legs on figures—these are open shapes. In sculpture, the shapes of the shadows form a part of the composition also. In any ceramic creation, all its masses, or component shapes, should be studied from all angles in relation to one another. They should be arranged to form a perfect balance.

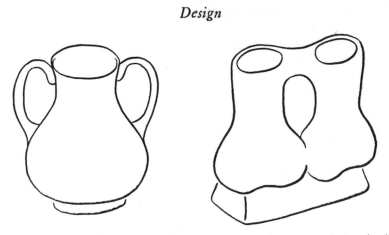

Above are examples of symmetrical arrangements of masses. Notice the balance in the relationship between the open and solid shapes in each of the illustrations.

The cat above is an example of an asymmetrical composition. Beside it is a sketch showing the basic masses of which it is composed. The perfect balance achieved by the arrangement of these masses makes this figure look very solid. Something more than balance, however, is required to give the arrangement life.

Movement

Movement is the element in design which leads the eye into looking at every part of the composition. Movement may be achieved by:

1. *Opposition.* The direction of a mass may be so forceful as to require an opposite movement in another mass to counterbalance it. This is clearly illustrated in the above right-hand sketch where the two prop-like masses are placed in opposition to counteract the powerful direction of the oval mass of the body.

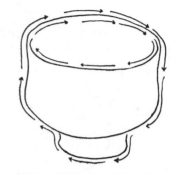

2. *Line.* In the silhouette of a piece of pottery one can see the line which moves from the base, up the side, around the rim, across and down the other side, across the base, and back to the starting point. In a figure, line should move not only around the silhouette, but also penetrate in and around the figure, thus integrating all the masses into a unified whole. In the illustration of the cat, notice how the line leads in and out and back again into the composition, causing one mass to flow into another. The design that the moving line makes should be kept simple, or it becomes too confusing to the eye.

3. *Light and Dark.* The eye moves instinctively from one light mass to another. It does the same with the dark masses. Therefore, a good composition should have a pleasing pattern of lights and darks which would lead the eye to the most important features of the composition. Patterns of lights and darks may be achieved through the shadows and prominences created by the manner in which the figure is modeled. Light and dark patterns may also be achieved by the decoration which may be put on the surface through color, applied design, incised line, or any of the other decorative methods.

4. *Repetition.* Masses or design motifs may be repeated to form a pattern of movement. The plate design illustrated here has a powerful horizontal and vertical movement (opposition), but the four repeats of the motif in each corner carry the eye around the circle which is the basic shape of the plate. (Prehistoric pottery from Coclé, Panama.)

Rhythm

Just as music must have rhythm which appeals to the ear, design must have rhythm to appeal to the eye. The relationship of space in which the masses or motifs are placed, and the manner in which the line moves throughout the composition create rhythm. The bowl illustrated to the right is a good example of a fine rhythmic design; made by an Arizona Indian.

Variety

Variety is the "spice" of design. It is the element which creates interest. Variety is achieved by making a slight change in the shape or line of the repeated mass or motif. It may also be gotten by varying slightly the intervals of space in which the motifs or masses are repeated; or by varying the light, shade, or color treatments of the mass or motif. Here is a simple example of the use of variety in design. The three leaves in the center are all of the same character. Each is of different length, however, and there are slight differences in the spaces between them. There is variety also in the shape and spacing of the petals of the flowers. More subtlety and variety in design are possible in handmade ceramics than those made by machine. That is the special charm of handcraft.

In Chinese, Japanese, and primitive art, the element of variety in design is used with great subtlety. That is also true of the fine design in Persian rugs.

Illustrated here is a vase made in recent times by the Acoma Indians of New Mexico. It is made of white clay and decorated in red and dark brown slip. The vase was biscuit-fired and then waxed. The design is charming in its variety.

Contrast

Contrast is another means of adding interest to form and decoration. Contrast may be achieved through the following combinations:

1. Light against dark effects: Black and white or light color against dark (as in sgraffito). In a figure, through light and shadow as created by modeling. Through raised or incised decoration.

2. Textures: Very interesting and beautiful effects can be gotten by combining glazed and unglazed areas in a composition; a glossy, runny glaze over parts of a matt glaze. This makes a contrast of a smooth, shiny surface against a dull surface. It may be used very successfully on the rims of bowls or vases. The glaze fires as though tear drops were running down from the rim. Rough textured against smooth textured biscuit-ware. Transparent glaze and an opaque mottled glaze.

Emotion

Consciously or subconsciously, people react emotionally to design. The reaction may be pleasant or unpleasant, a happy or an unhappy experience to the beholder. Often he may not know why.

There are universal laws which govern the emotional reaction to design. A pattern in which the horizontal predominates will evoke a feeling of calm and peace. Where the dominant theme is of lines crossing each other, there is a sensation of opposition, conflict, or great action. The vertical gives a feeling of strength. An upward curve imparts a sensation of uplift, as in the gothic curve seen in many churches. A downward curve may express sadness.

A good design requires a well-balanced arrangement of several types of lines or movements, with one of them dominating the complete design. Too many movements or lines in the same direction would be monotonous and throw the composition off balance. Compare interest and movements of lines in above designs.

The square as a shape is static and lifeless, because it is equal on all sides. So is the rectangle which is built on a double square. In designing shapes based on these geometric forms, therefore, make them either larger than a square or smaller than a double square. Compare placement of design in illustrations below.

If the design is placed in the direct center, it makes the shape appear as though it were cleaved in two. To preserve a feeling of unity, it is better to place the design somewhere off center.

The design always reflects the tensity or freedom with which it was applied. Compare the conventional designs on formal dinnerware with the gay, free designs of peasant ware such as the Quimper, made in France; compare both with the highly cultured freedom of some of the Chinese and Japanese designs.

To sum up, the principles of good design are: function, structure, balance, movement (opposition, line, light and dark masses, repetition), rhythm, variety, contrast, and emotion.

No one of these principles can be singled out as the most important. What is very important, however, is that they are all interrelated to form the unified composition, just as all the physical parts of the human body are interrelated with the mental, emotional, and spiritual to form the complete man or woman.

Many people find that, as they are creating, this interrelationship arises instinctively. That is good. It is also good to be aware that a well-designed ceramic piece must not look as though it were made of a rigid material like metal or wood. Its appearance must retain the plastic quality characteristic of clay. The decoration should be kept simple. It should be subordinated and integrated into the basic shape. The final product should give joy to the hands that touch it, pleasure to the eyes that look upon it, and comfort to the one who uses it.

The refined, cultured beauty of the ancient Chinese and Persian ceramics; the rugged, primitive beauty of the work of the African Negroes and the Indians of all the Americas; the peasant pottery and the elegant, sophisticated wares of the ancient and not so ancient European potters: these are among the things which will speak eternally to man of man's struggle for perfection.

In the following pages are renderings of ceramics made by people of various cultures, places, and times. In them is a wealth of inspiration for the student who is willing to study them, to learn how and why they were made; and to learn to apply to his own creations the same honesty, love, and patience with which these beautiful things were made. The student will soon realize that when he achieves a perfect piece, his joy repays him for whatever labor or disappointment its creation may have entailed.

Courtesy of American Museum of Natural History, New York City

The mugs on the previous page were dug up from the Aztec ruins in New Mexico. Notice the crude, primitive shapes, the way the handles are attached to the bodies, and the well-organized and rich designs.

To the right is a storage jar made by a modern Indian in the San Ildefonso Pueblo in the southwestern region of the United States.

Courtesy of American Museum of Natural History, New York City

ARIZONA INDIAN POTTERY. DESIGN INSPIRED BY A PARROT

Courtesy of U. S. National Museum, Smithsonian Institute, Wash., D. C.

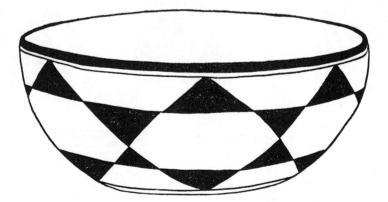

This bowl was made by an American Indian of New Mexico. Note how the triangles which form the six-pointed star are placed to conform with the shape of the bowl.

This ancient Peruvian pottery is now in the American Museum of Natural History. The bird design on the top piece and the spider on the bottom are both striking examples of the use of contrast, repetition and variety in design. Because the motifs are conventionalized, they are far more effectively decorative than if they had been drawn realistically.

Courtesy of American Museum of Natural History, New York City

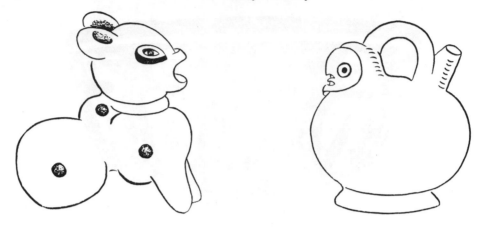

A small toy whistle (about 3" x 4") in the form of a cat. From ancient Mexico. The basic shapes of this toy are 3 balls: the head, the chest, and the back.

A jug with drinking spout, combining sculpture with pottery. From ancient Peru.

ANCIENT MEXICAN POTTERY

Courtesy of American Museum of Natural History, New York City

Cat. no.
14/5150

Cat. no.
14/6066

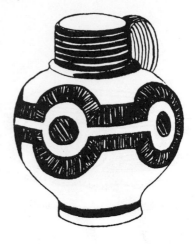

The five pieces on page 103 were made in prehistoric times. They were found in the Coclé province of Panama. Notice how the basic shapes of the pottery, the conventionalized sculptured ornaments, and the decorative designs are all fused into a unified harmony. The basic shape is dominant while all the elements of decoration are subjugated for the embellishment of the shape. This type of design may be carried out by slip painting and sgraffito. (The catalogued pieces are reproduced through the courtesy of the Museum of the American Indian, Heye Foundation, New York City.)

Three jugs made by the Bakamba tribe (Middle Congo) of Africa. This pottery was found about 1895 and is now in the Musée de l'Homme in Paris. The shapes and designs are powerful in their simplicity. The designs are applied in dark brown over a white clay body. The applied designs are incised.

PEASANT POTTERY FROM PORTUGAL

The above renderings are based on illustrations by de Paulo in *Quelques Images de l'Art*.

This ancient pottery is in the Candia Museum in Crete. The elegance of shape and design speak eloquently of the highly developed civilization attained there several thousand years ago. The designs are very rhythmic and beautifully integrated into the pottery shapes. Decorations such as these are done by slip painting and sgraffito.

A pitcher and two albarelli (jars for storing medicines) in Italian majolica. The body of this ware is usually of a light or dark colored clay which is covered with a white enamel glaze containing tin oxide. Over the unfired glaze the design is painted in underglaze colors. This requires well-controlled brush work.

The three illustrations of Italian Majolica are from Guilio Ferrari's *Review of Ancient and Modern Art of All Countries*. Torino, C. Crudo & Co., Italy.

Though these pieces of pottery are similar in the nature of their design, one was made 5000 years before the other. In each case a slip tracer was used to trail a light slip over a dark body. Above is a predynastic Egyptian bowl. (Courtesy of the Brooklyn Museum.) Below is a twentieth century bowl from Andalucia, Spain. (Courtesy of the Hispanic Society of America, New York City.)

Cat. no.
70/14331-2

A teapot and vase from China. The dignified
grace and beauty of the basic shapes of this pottery are enhanced by the applied design.

Courtesy of American Museum of Natural History, New York City

Cat. no.
70/13052

Early nineteenth century Pennsylvania Dutch plate.

From the *American Index of Design.* Courtesy of the National Gallery of Art, Washington, D. C.

Pennsylvania Dutch Plate in the collections of the Metropolitan Museum of Art, New York City.

Design on a Pennsylvania Dutch plate, in the collections of the Metropolitan Museum of Art, New York City. The body of this plate was made of dark clay which was covered with a coat of white slip. The design was done with sgraffito and slip painting. This technique was typical of Pennsylvania Dutch pottery.

Every ceramist should take pride in designing his own monogram to be used as an identification of his work. In pottery, the monogram is usually placed on the underside of the bottom. In sculpture, it is placed in an inconspicuous spot where it will not interfere with the general design.

CHAPTER TEN

Ceramics for Children   *A Guide for Parents and Teachers*

MOST children take to clay with an instinctive, natural ease. If teacher or parent provides the proper guidance, the time the child spends in clay work will be charged with joyous concentration.

Such joy in working is very precious. If not nurtured, it may be killed. The parent or teacher should try to guide the child toward the expression and realization of his own ideas. To impose a rigid course upon the child, ignoring his preferences, is by all means to be avoided.

To illustrate: one classroom was constantly conducted in a single group. Three tables were set together to make a single long one. All the children were seated around this table with the teacher at the head. She was explaining her method of building a duck. The children were required to follow her directions step by step. Result—a majority of the children were bored and more interested in what was going on outside the windows.

In another classroom, the tables were separated, with three or four children sitting at each table. The teacher was giving individual guidance to the children who were busy making what they wanted. Where several children wished to make things which required the same technique (such as coil, slab, etc.), she grouped them together. She showed them the method. From there they proceeded to make whatever objects they desired. In the course of their work, if they reached a place where they needed help to go on, the teacher came to their assistance. Result—interest was at a keen pitch and the children were disappointed when the session ended.

This joy in constructive activity is the dominant factor which should be preserved.

To encourage the child to work as he prefers does not mean that carelessness and sloppy work should be permitted. On the contrary, the child must be given the incentive to feel pride in a thing that is neatly and well done.

Children should be able to look forward to clay work as a time for general relaxation, a time of release from the usual unavoidable tensions to which they are subjected.

"In school, all day, we are not permitted to talk, but here we may. It's such fun," said one little girl. A pleasant conversational atmosphere is conducive to a flowing freedom of expression and to happy, creative work. Sometimes what the children are doing will remind them of a song and they will start to sing spontaneously. It creates a sense of unity for parent or teacher to join in the fun, provided it is kept within the bounds of consideration and orderliness so that disturbance to others is avoided

Most children, when coming into clay class, are filled with enthusiastic ideas of what they want to make. It would be a grave error for the parent or teacher to deflect them except for those ideas unsuitable to clay. Young boys, for instance, often want to make guns and knives. In that case it should be explained that such things are made better in metal. These children should be guided into choosing something more suitable.

What do children want to make? All children want to make things which represent some purpose to them. The purpose may be related to real people and experiences, or it may relate to the people and experiences in their imaginations.

Anne Marie is making a bowl for Pinky, her friend's cat. Peter is going to portray his dog, Noributch, drinking her milk. Carol Anne is making a covered dish for her mother's birthday. Susan, a six-year-old, is making a figure of a little girl wearing a bridal veil, as she sees herself in fantasy on some remotely future wedding day. Gary is making a dinosaur which he saw on a visit to the Museum of Natural History. Soon the material fashioned by those busy fingers is transformed into something of much more significance than the humble clay, for it becomes imbued with all the thought of play and whimsy that these lively imaginations impart to it.

Sometimes a child will ask, "What shall I make?" This is an opportunity to help him explore his fund of real and imaginative experiences and to evoke in him new awarenesses and evaluations of such experiences. Suggestions for inspiration may be gotten by discussing with the child the things he saw or did at camp, at the zoo, a picnic, the circus, during play period, at home, in school, or on a nature walk. Through such conversation and suggestion, the child may be stimulated into an enthusiastic desire to translate these experiences into clay.

About once in every four or five lessons the children may welcome a group lesson. Even then, two or three among them may wish to work on their own ideas. They should be permitted to do so provided they sit quietly at a table in a corner of the room to avoid distracting the group.

What should parents expect their children to accomplish with clay work? Should they expect them to become great craftsmen or artists? Should they expect a piece of fine workmanship to result from every lesson? Should they feel that unless the child has a great talent for this craft, it is a waste of time and money? Should they feel disappointed if Billy or Sally has but one humble little bowl or figure to show for all the time put into the course? To all these questions the answer is "No."

As in painting, music or dancing, the great positive values in clay work for the child are these:

1. It helps him build up confidence in his own powers.
2. It helps to develop any latent talents he may have.
3. It creatively channels his excess energy.
4. It provides the means to give play to his imagination.
5. It develops a deftness of hand and a sensitivity to good form.

6. It strengthens the coordination between the hand and the eye.

7. It gives him an elementary understanding of the nature of matter all around him.

8. It gives him a sense of release from many unavoidable tensions such as crowded living quarters or classrooms, or the many disciplines which are necessarily imposed upon him in the course of the day's happenings.

9. It helps to liberate him from many of his own inner fears and inhibitions.

10. It helps him constructively in his mental and emotional development.

11. It stimulates his sense of awareness and well-being and broadens his understanding of himself in relation to his friends and the world around him.

The parents should be willing to accept the results of the child's efforts as a tangible expression of his inner life and growth. It is well for the parent to realize that the proper development of the child is of prime importance; the development of the craftsman comes as a by-product. If the child is enthusiastic about his work, it is a sign that such development is taking place.

Once in a while, a child will be found who shows a very unusual aptitude and love for this craft. In such a case, parent and teacher should give the child all the help they can to prepare himself adequately for what may well become his future life's work.

Here are some helpful suggestions for parents and teachers:

1. Have a definite place for every tool and for all material and equipment.

2. Keep everything where it will be easily accessible to the children.

3. Teach them where each item is to be found and its use. Train them to respect the tools and materials they work with; to get the tools and clay by themselves when they need them, and to return everything to its proper place when they are through. This gives them a sense of freedom as well as of responsibility.

4. Train them to wear aprons and to be neat about their work.

5. Teach them to clean their tools and tables after every lesson.

6. Guide the young children (up to the age of about 8) to make simple things so that the forming can be completed in one lesson. The decorating is done in the next lesson.

7. Teach them to cooperate with one another in the sharing and use of tools and material.

8. Have all materials such as clay, slip, and engobes ready for use.

9. Since the child is apt to drop things accidentally, avoid glass water containers. Aluminum cups, heavy paper cups, or empty milk cartons with the tops cut off are preferable.

10. Utilize shelves or some other area in the home or classroom to display the child's finished wares. This integrates the child's creative efforts with the society around him, and adds to his pleasure and satisfaction in his work.

11. For ideal conditions, one teacher should handle no more than 10 to 15 children.

12. Show the children pieces of clay in the various stages and explain their uses:

plasteline, dry powdered pottery clay, slip, moist plastic clay, leather-hard clay, bone-dry clay (show how fragile it is and how carefully this stage must be handled), biscuit fired clay, and a piece of glazed ware.

13. Expose the children to fine ceramics by taking them to the museums and borrowing picture collections from the libraries and museums.

In the classroom children should be grouped according to age levels.

Four- and Five-year-olds

At this age, the child enjoys exploring the feel of the clay: its moisture, its look, its texture, the shape left in it by his pressing palm and fingers. He should be guided into making various imaginative figures from the abstract shapes that his hand squeezes into the clay. These shapes can be used as paper weights or made into book ends. He can be taught to roll the clay into small coils and slabs and to press designs into the clay with fingers or tools. He can be shown how to make an oval or rectangular tile into which he is to press an imprint of his hand. This makes an ashtray or wall plaque which any parent will cherish. Leaves, berries, or small twigs may also be used for tiles. (Leaves may be left in the clay because they burn out in the firing.)

There should be very little emphasis on technique, but there should be general guidance in the use of materials, neatness, and the care of tools, as well as in the importance of sharing equipment and being helpful to one another. This discipline which working with clay requires helps develop the child's concepts of good citizenship, responsibility, and consideration in working with others.

No fuss or worry should be made about a little clay getting onto clothes, since it washes out very easily. When dry, it can be brushed off with a stiff brush. The usual working period for children of four to five is 45 to 60 minutes.

Six- and Seven-year-olds

At the ages of six and seven, the child is taught how and why to wedge his clay. He should be trained to get materials and tools for himself from the shelves and to clean and put them back where they belong when the lesson is over.

He should be shown how to make simple objects using the coil and slab methods (see pp. 23 and 31): a cup, an ashtray, a tile, a bowl, a pitcher, etc.

Parent or teacher may prepare simple patterns, made of cardboard, to be used on slabs. The card shapes, hearts, diamonds, clubs and spades, are generally favorites for ashtrays. These shapes are cut out of the slabs of clay. A coil of clay is attached around the edge of the shape and a rest for the cigarette is pressed into one corner with the thumb.

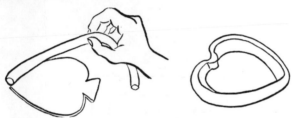

Using a large maple leaf as a pattern on a slab of clay the child may make a leaf dish as follows:

1. Cut leaf out of clay slab ¼″ thick.
2. Remove excess clay.
3. Draw vein markings into the leaf.
4. Make a ring out of a coil of clay 1″ thick.
5. Place leaf inside the ring and gently press the center down. The sides of the clay leaf will turn up against the ring to form a dish.
6. Smooth the edges all around the leaf with the fingers.
7. Attach stem to leaf curled into the shape of a handle.
8. Remove leaf dish from ring when leather-hard.

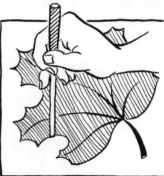

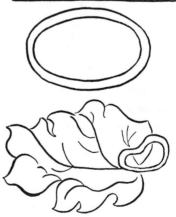

The child may shape the clay into a solid mass, then form a figure by carving with a tool. When almost leather-hard it should be hollowed out. Small details such as ears and tail are added to the form.

This method is good for seated or crouching figures.

If he should wish to make an animal with standing or separated legs, he may be shown the method described on page 39. Children usually get a great deal of fine, natural rhythm and movement into figures with this method.

Children in this group may use colored slip for decorating their wares. The usual working period is one hour.

Eight- Nine- and Ten-year-olds

At this age children should be given the responsibility of cleaning their tools as well as their
tables. While younger children are too intrigued
by the experience of handling clay and the thrill
of creating to be critical of results, the child of
eight begins to look upon his work with a dis-
cerning eye. He will have the desire to strive for
more detail and better workmanship. He should
be given elementary instruction in design. Parent
or teacher should never give idle praise because
the child is quick to sense it and just as quick to
resent it. Everything good in his work should be
lauded, however, and whatever needs to be criti-
cized should be pointed up as a way of improving
what has already been done.

This group may attempt objects requiring
more than one period. The children should be
shown how to wrap their work to keep it moist
until the next lesson (see p. 19). They may
make slightly more advanced objects in the coil,
animal, and slab methods. With the last, the
child can form little houses or cottages which
can be used as banks. By this method, covered
boxes, dishes and jars can also be produced.
Coils can be used for making a log cabin.

This age group should be taught to use colored slip for sgraffito and slip painting to decorate their pieces. It should also learn to use
incised lines and applied designs. (See chapter
on decoration.)

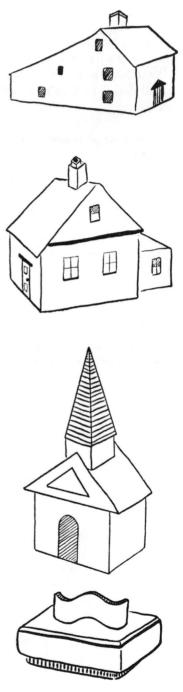

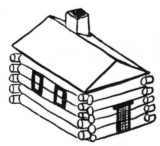

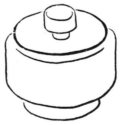

Another good technique for children of this age is the sectional method. It lends itself well to the occasional group lesson.

1. Draw the plan of a simple figure on paper.

2. Divide the figure into geometric sections.

3. Show children how to roll balls, cylinders, and triangles to form the various sections separately, and join them with thick adhesion slip.

4. Figure should be trimmed and smoothed when leather-hard.

5. Decorate with colored slip.

The usual working period for eight- to ten-year-olds is 1½ hours.

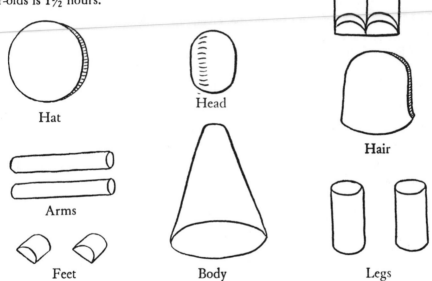

Hat

Head

Hair

Arms

Feet

Body

Legs

Eleven- and Twelve-year-olds

Children at this age should assume all the previously mentioned responsibilities. They should also be given simple tasks in helping the teacher with preparations of materials. They may work with all the methods previously mentioned, but a higher standard of workmanship should be expected of them. They may be taught to use the slip tracer in addition to the simpler types of decoration. (See p. 56.) They should be taught how to mix plaster and make a simple, one-piece mold of a bowl or a tile. (See pp. 44–45.) They should be shown how to do slip casting as well as press casting. (See pp. 51–53.)

Children up to the age of twelve should not be permitted to handle glaze. Glaze materials are very harmful if they get into the mouth, nose, or open cuts in the skin. Young children, absorbed in their work, often put their fingers near mouth or nose unconsciously. Glazes for ware made by younger children should be applied by the teacher or parent.

Thirteen-year-olds and Over

Children. in this group may be taught glaze mixing and glaze application. (See chapter on glaze.) They may be taught how to decorate with underglaze (p. 59) and how to use the pottery wheel (p. 40). They may help with stacking the kiln (p. 78) and gradually work into the responsibility of stacking the kiln completely by themselves; similarly with the firing. The period of apprenticeship under supervision, however, should be long and thorough because of the potential dangers to the child and the possible damage to the ware.

Children of all age groups should be given an understanding of the complete ceramic process. They should, if possible, be given an opportunity to see a kiln in the process of being stacked for firing and also of being fired.

In the Home

The mother whose child is making ceramics at home will find it convenient to set aside one shelf in a closet or chest for all material and equipment, which need not consist of any more than the following:

a. 5 to 10 lbs. moist clay. (Store in a covered crock or other rustproof covered container. Add a little water once in a while to keep clay moist.)

b. 18″ square of oilcloth.

c. 18″ length of 1″ doweling stick.

d. 1 or 2 medium-sized water color brushes.

e. ¼ lb. each of 3 or 4 colored engobes. Yellow, blue, brown, black and white are a good choice. These can be purchased in powdered form and made ready for use by adding enough water to form a creamy consistency.

f. 1 small, dull kitchen paring knife.

g. 1 modeling tool (one end to have a wire ferrule).

h. 1 small elephant's ear sponge.

i. 1 flexible steel scraper.

j. 1 lb. transparent clear glaze.

A tin breadbox makes an ideal "damp" closet for keeping work moist. In many cases a small electric test kiln is purchased for the child's use. Such a kiln is as simple to operate as an electric iron. It plugs into any electric outlet and costs approximately $24.00.

For the child who is home from school while convalescing from illness, clay work is one of the happiest of pastimes. The creative absorption of this work can actually hasten his complete recovery.

The pliant nature of clay, its ability to yield to the softest touch as well as to the most vigorous pounding, and the ease with which it can be fashioned, destroyed and refashioned make it ideal for the happy, well-adjusted child. It is also an excellent means of expression and stabilization for the child who stammers, for the child who is nervous, timid or unsocial, for the child who is pampered with too much attention, or the one who does not get enough. Children often find it easier to express in clay what they find too difficult to put into words. It has been demonstrated that the emotional release they find in clay work factually helps their restoration to a sense of security and happiness.

Clay work is also used very successfully with children to prevent or correct delinquency. It has been found that a large number of delinquents are children who have been starved emotionally and denied a sense of security because of unfortunate living conditions. Others may be highly gifted children who were never given a constructive outlet for their creative energies. Clay work is one of the means used very effectively to reeducate such children into the positive values of love instead of hate, and of creation instead of destruction.

In the Classroom

On the next page is a plan for a space-saving cabinet for classroom use. It was designed for and is being used in the ceramic studio of the Riverdale Neighborhood House, New York City.

On six feet of wall, storage space is provided for all tools, equipment, and materials. It also has closet space for aprons, a bin for rags and pieces of oilcloth, closets for record and attendance books, reference materials, and picture collections. Everything is so arranged that any child easily may reach whatever he needs.

It is made of lumber 12″ wide. The diagonally shaded areas have doors on the front to make the closets. The horizontally shaded area is a board 12″ wide by 10″ high, nailed across the front of the shelf to make a box-like bin in which to keep the rags and oilcloth. The unshaded areas are open shelves.

A classroom should also have a "damp" closet for storing unfinished ware which must be kept moist. This closet should have plaster bats about 1½″ to 2″ thick covering its shelves. The bats are soaked in water so that they retain moisture for a number of days, thus keeping the atmosphere damp inside the closet.

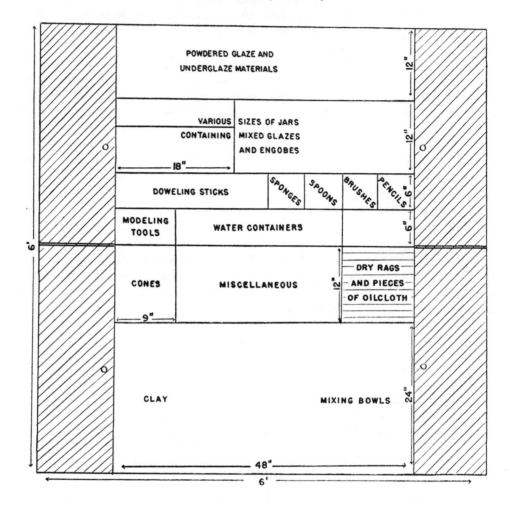

CHAPTER ELEVEN

Ceramics in Occupational Therapy

*"Open our eyes to the nobility of life
and its sacred opportunities for service."*
HEBREW PRAYER.

INHERENT in every human being is the instinct for usefulness, the desire to be of use to others as well as to oneself.

This instinct functions in many different and interrelated ways: physically, socially, economically, mentally, emotionally, spiritually. When any of these functions of usefulness is denied through injury or repression, the first normal reaction is to try to regain it and become a complete being again.

Many are able to do this by themselves; others require help. This is the area where occupational therapy has become a necessary and recognized profession.

As a profession, it received great impetus in this country in 1918 when General Pershing ordered one thousand Reconstruction Aides in Occupational Therapy to be sent overseas for his wounded soldiers in the American Expeditionary Forces. He knew that a person suffering from illness or disability of any sort is beset with the fear of never being able to *do* things again, and that this fear may become more detrimental than the condition itself. He understood that injury to body, mind, or soul responds quickly to the restorative treatment of a creative occupation, and that absorption in such work dispels fears, tensions, and melancholy.

From the sad experiences of war, we have learned the value of occupational therapy in civilian life where hazards are abundant. Occupational therapy has now become a necessary and recognized profession and is making a fine record of achievement.

A trained occupational therapist is equipped and able, in most cases, to restore people to a sense of whole and happy living even where there is almost complete frustration or helplessness.

Part of the training consists of studying the necessary movements as well as the sensory and psychological effects involved in the performance of various occupations, arts, and crafts. They also study the person as a complete being: his strength, his weakness, his talents, his personality, his injury, his special needs. On this basis, they assign the most suitable activity.

As the individual improves, the activity and length of work period are changed to meet his new requirements. One whose fingers were injured, for instance, will be given the mildest form of manual activity just as soon as he is ready for it. As the muscles and nerves gain in strength, he will be offered something which requires a little more resistance and a longer work period. Thus the activity and time are graded until the maximum benefit is derived.

Activities are generally chosen with three basic aims:

Psychological. To divert the individual's thoughts from himself and his troubles, and to help him spend his leisure time constructively and enjoyably.

Functional. To restore function to injured parts by increasing joint motion, muscle strength, and coordination; also to aid in mental rehabilitation.

Pre-vocational. To explore aptitudes and build up endurance and dexterity for the individual's return to such employment as is suitable for his condition and personality.

Enjoyment and interest are basic to successful occupational therapy, the purpose of which is to integrate the individual's sense of unified well-being. To achieve this, the creative arts have been found to be a most satisfactory method. For when a person is given the means of free, creative expression and when his head, hand, and heart are preoccupied with the universal principles of design (see chapter on design), he derives the most satisfaction.

Among the arts, clay has proven itself to be one of the most valuable of media because it is three dimensional, it appeals to touch and to sight, it produces results which are esthetic as well as utilitarian, and it lends itself well to a graded variety of movements, force, and resistance. The fact that clay can be shaped and reshaped until the most desired form is attained is associated psychologically with man's innate desire to pull himself out of chaos into order, out of misery into happiness. These are some of the factors which impart to clay work its ability to restore, heal, and bring to man a feeling of inner unity and peace.

As part of the psychological aim of occupational therapy, the sheer joy of creating with clay and of being able to make things which are useful and beautiful promote a wholesome mental attitude and provide an outlet for the release of such negative emotions as anger, fear, jealousy, or insecurity.

In the functional aim, there are many specific uses for which clay is ideal. All the hand-building methods offer a broad variety of movements and touch, from the most delicate to that requiring much force or resistance. When a person is confined to bed rest, he is able to enjoy the use of clay with a minimum of tools and noise. Dr. William Rush Denton, Jr. in his book, "Prescribing Occupational Therapy" (p. 113), quotes Dr. Philip K. Brown, specialist in the treatment of tuberculosis, as saying, "For any patient, even those confined to bed, pottery is the best single occupation found."

Some nerve or muscle injuries in the hand, wrist, or arm, such as may result from polio or burns, require special exercises to build up their bending power; others require strengthening of their power to stretch or twist. All these needs can be met within the gamut of movements in clay work, such as wedging, rolling slabs or coils, joining, smoothing, modeling, forming texture, squeezing, pushing, pinching, or pounding.

When the nerves of the hand are in the process of healing, the hand may be very sensitive and painful to touch. In such cases, the finer, delicate movements involved in the making of light pieces of ceramic jewelry, especially the shaping and smoothing of petals, are very beneficial.

As more strength develops, rolling small slabs of clay, modeling small figurines, pressing clay into molds, and tile-making will afford a little more resistance.

Wedging, casting, and making large pieces of pottery or sculpture by the coil method or any other hand-building method are excellent when even greater movement, force, and resistance are required.

Decorating by slip painting, sgraffito, incised or embossed line and applied design is not only good for developing the range of motion, but is also excellent for achieving finer coordination.

While the hand-building methods are beneficial for injuries to the upper limbs, the pottery kick wheel is very useful for strengthening the lower extremities, *i.e.*, the hip, knee or ankle.

In the field of psychiatry, clay work is valuable because the mental and emotional absorption it evokes makes it a perfect medium for the most personal self-expression.

In the pre-vocational aim ceramics is being used as a means of developing manual dexterity, coordination, and in building up work tolerance for the individual's return to his previous occupation wherever it is possible and desirable, or his placement in some other occupation more suited to his needs.

It often happens that during illness, at home or in the hospital, a person discovers new talents which he never knew he possessed because he was always too busy to uncover them. Such discoveries may effect vast changes in people's lives. There are cases of individuals who have become so fascinated with ceramics that they decided to adopt it as a vocation in place of their previous work.

There seem to be two schools of thought among doctors as to the use of clay for arthritics and people injured by burns. Some physicians approve of it while others disapprove because of the dampness in the clay. In many cases where it has been tried, however, it has been found to be beneficial as a mild form of exercising the taut skin and muscles of the fingers. Those were cases of people who did not seem to be sensitive to the dampness in the clay.

Clay work often helps elderly people discover new capacities for creative expression within themselves which they never knew existed. This opens up new horizons to them.

For the blind there is no better medium to develop the concepts of planes, form, texture, design, and space. A large portion of knowledge is acquired through the sense of touch. Clay, with its various tactile qualities, is ideal especially for those who were born sightless or who lost their sight at too early an age to have many memories of the visible world. Their understanding of things and people is made more keen through work with clay.

Mrs. Theresa Nova Bader, herself only partially sighted, teaches ceramics to the blind at the N. Y. Guild for the Jewish Blind. She says, "To be able to create a beautiful, finished product completely and independently is a great satisfaction to us. And what a joy it is when we take our creations home and use them in our daily living. We make all sorts of things for the home, such as cups and saucers, bowls, lamp bases, book ends, ashtrays, jam jars, cigarette boxes, and many others. The fact that we have no sight makes most of our work very original since there is very little likelihood for copying. We are guided chiefly by imagination and touch, and the quality of our work is very high, sometimes superior to that of people with vision. Though we use the coil method chiefly, we are also able to use all the other methods of forming, including casting and the pottery wheel. We also do our own decorating and glazing."

Following are a few representative cases where ceramics was used successfully as a form of occupational therapy:

A little girl was born with Erbs Palsy, a nerve injury which paralyzed her upper extremities. She could not move her fingers, pronate her hand (turn it palm down), or bend her elbow. She was started on occupational therapy at the age of about three. She began with the lightest of paper crafts and was led into playing with clay. At the age of about seven she was able to use her fingers well enough to model clay figurines of which she was very proud. Movement in the injured parts has been restored to the point where now, at the age of eleven, she is able to enjoy riding a bicycle.

A veteran with osteomyelitis (a severe infection of the bone) in his leg was confined to the hospital for over a year. He had to spend most of his time either in bed or in a wheelchair. In civilian life he had been employed at a racetrack and had never had a creative hobby in his life. He was sent to the ceramics class in the hospital and he came reluctantly. In a few days he had made a perfectly formed cream pitcher. After that he could not be kept away from the class. His next project was a covered sugar bowl and then a figurine of his pet dog who devotedly waited for him at home. He worked meticulously and was satisfied only after the form was perfected. This man started ceramics as a diversion but it opened a new world of esthetic experiences to him.

One veteran had a spinal cord injury which paralyzed his upper and lower extremities. He could not open his fist from a tightly clenched position because of contractures. He was able to feed himself and perform other self-care functions only with great difficulty. He had no interest in any craft because he felt his hands could not possibly do anything requiring much motion or skill. He was finally persuaded to try ceramics. He began by pounding a piece of clay with his fist and then pressing it into a mold. The first project was a small tile. He decorated it by holding the brush between his index and middle fingers and obtained very fine results. He was then taught to build with coils. Pieces of clay were broken off for him at first. Later he was able to do this himself. He rolled the coils with the exposed part of his palm and was able to execute this with great skill. At the time of his discharge from the hospital, he had completed a beer mug of which he was justly proud. He hoped to continue doing ceramics as a hobby. He is a machinist by trade.

Another veteran has been confined to the hospital for about four years, during which time he has had to undergo a series of operations on his leg. He started working with ceramics. He loved it and became so expert that he decided to do it professionally. From time to time he is sent home on leave for a period of several weeks. His family set up a workshop and kiln for him and when he is home he is able to sell almost everything he makes.

These are times when the world is suffering the birth-pangs of the realization of the "One World." Vast human resources are being wasted through war and disease; minds are befogged by fear, hate, and other obsessions. Sensibilities are being deadened through manufactured and decadent diversions.

These are the times to take inventory of those things which have the power to restore and replenish man's will to live and create constructively; and the power to release man from his many torments so that he may feel free to use life's "sacred opportunities for service" for himself and his fellow-men.

Such precious powers are vested in the creative arts, not the least of which is the art of the humble piece of clay.

Sources of Supplies
Bibliography
Glossary

Sources of Supplies

Most ceramic supply companies mail catalogues upon request. Such catalogues provide considerable information of use to the ceramist.

General Ceramic Supplies and Equipment:

California
L. H. Butcher Co.
Los Angeles, Cal.

Braun-Knecht-Heimann Co.
1400 16 Street
San Francisco, Cal.

Canada
The E. Harris Co., Ltd.
73 King Street, East
Toronto 1, Ontario.

Colorado
Denver Fire Clay Co.
P. O. Box 5510
Denver 17, Colorado.

Indiana
American Art Clay Co.
Indianapolis 24, Ind.

Maryland
Pottery Arts Supply Co.
2552 Greenmount Ave.
Baltimore 18, Md.

New Jersey
Specialized Ceramic Corp.
Arlington & West 3rd St.
Plainfield, N. J.

New York
B. F. Drakenfeld & Co., Inc.
45 Park Place
New York 7, N. Y.

Jack D. Wolfe Co., Inc.
62 Horatio St.
New York 14, N. Y.

Stewart Clay Co.
133 Mulberry St.
New York, N. Y.

Buffalo Ceramic Center
76 Allen Street
Buffalo 2, N. Y.

Ohio
Harrop Ceramic Service
35 E. Gay St.
Columbus 15, O.

George Fetzer
1205 17th Ave.
Columbus, O.

Allied Engineering Division
Ferro Enamel Corp.
4150 E. 56 St.
Cleveland 5, O.

Pennsylvania
W. H. Fairchild
712 Centre St.
Freeland, Pa.

Damerell Mfg. Co.
Swedesford Road,
Exton, Pa.

Ceramic Color and Chemical Mfg. Co.
New Brighton, Pa.

O. Hommel Co.
Pittsburgh 30, Pa.

Kilns:

Bell Ceramics, Inc.
Dept. C, 21 Midland Ave.
Montclair, N. J.

Harper Electric Furnace Corp.
39 River St., Buffalo 2, N. Y.

L. & L. Manufacturing Co.
804 Mulberry St.
Upland, Pa.

Petterson Multi-Unit Kilns
1007 S. Acacia St.
Compton, Cal.

Rogers Electric Kilns
Glenside, Pa.

Ceramic Supplies and Materials:

Industrial Arts Cooperative Service, Inc.
340 Amsterdam Avenue
New York City.

American Handicrafts Co., Inc.
45–49 S. Harrison St.
East Orange, N. J.
and
12 East 41 St.
New York 17, N. Y.

The general ceramic supply companies, in many cases, also sell kilns as well as pin backs, earring backs, and cement.

Bibliography

TECHNICAL:

Chinese Ceramic Glazes. By A. L. Hetherington—P. D. & Ione Perkins, South Pasadena, Calif., 1948.

The Potter's Craft. By Charles F. Binns—D. Van Nostrand Co., Inc., New York, N. Y. 3rd Edition, 1947.

Pottery Production Processes. By Ceramic Industry, 59 E. Van Buren St., Chicago 5, Ill.

Pottery. By George J. Cox—Macmillan, New York, N. Y., 1927.

A Potter's Book. By Bernard Leach—Faber and Faber, Ltd., London. American edition, 1946, Transatlantic Arts, Inc., Forest Hills, N. Y.

HISTORY AND APPRECIATION:

The Book of Pottery and Porcelain. 2 vols. By Warren E. Cox—Crown Publishers, New York, N. Y., 1944.

Pottery of the Europeans. By Helen E. Stiles—E. P. Dutton & Co., New York, N. Y., 1940.

Pottery of the United States. By Helen E. Stiles—E. P. Dutton & Co., 1941.

MAGAZINES:

Ceramic Age. 421 Parker St., Newark, N. J.

Craft Horizons. American Craftsmen's Cooperative Council, Inc., 485 Madison Ave., New York 22, N. Y.

PAMPHLETS:

Italian Majolica. By Victor Merlo.

Chinese Art. By Karl With.

Pottery & Porcelain. By George H. Opdyke.

These are published by Esto Publishing Co., P. O. Box 46, Pasadena, Cal. They are also sold in many art museums.

EDUCATIONAL AND CULTURAL:

Creative Re-Education. By Frederick Peterson, M. D.—G. P. Putnam's Sons, New York, N. Y., 1936.

Art and Regeneration. By Maria Petrie—Paul Elek, Publishers, Ltd., London, 1946.

Glossary

Ball clay—Very plastic clay. It is used to give plasticity to clay which is short.

Bat—A flat slab of plaster on which clay is formed. The plaster absorbs the moisture from the wet clay.

Bentonite—A highly plastic clay. A maximum of 2% is used to keep glazes from settling. Too much bentonite makes glaze shrink and peel.

Biscuit-ware—Unglazed clay which has been fired once.

Bone-dry—Complete dryness; the state at which the ware is fit to be set inside the kiln for firing.

Borax—A very strong flux used in glazes and frits.

Calcine—To heat a substance to a state where it can easily be pulverized.

China clay—Same as alumina or kaolin. Up to 25% will give opacity and a matt quality to a glaze. It withstands a very high temperature.

Colorants—Various oxides and carbonates which are able to withstand high temperatures, and are used to give color to glazes or clay bodies.

Cones—Cone-shaped pieces of clay used to measure the time and temperature at which the ware matures.

Cottle—A retaining wall placed around a model from which a plaster mold is to be made.

Deflocculent—A substance put into casting slip in order to keep it in suspension and of a smooth consistency.

Engobe—Colored slip used for decoration.

Feldspar—A widely found mineral of which there are several varieties. Orthoclase feldspar which contains potash is the one most frequently used in bodies and glazes. It produces density. When decomposed it becomes kaolin.

Flint—Silica, the addition of which gives porosity to clay or glaze.

Flux—A material which melts under heat thus providing the medium for the fusion of all the other materials which are contained in a glaze.

Frit—A mixture of soluble and insoluble glaze materials which have been calcined. The purpose of fritting is to change the soluble materials into insoluble form.

Greenware—Ware which is in its raw, unfired state.

Grog—Clay which has been biscuit-fired and finely ground; used to give clay porosity and texture and to decrease shrinkage and warping.

Gum tragacanth—A natural gum used in glazes and underglaze painting as an aid to adhesion to the ware at the time of application.

Kaolin—China clay.

Leather-hard—That state of clay which is still wet, yet too firm to bend.

Mahl-stick—A stick used for steadying the hands when turning ware on the wheel or decorating.

Overglaze—Mineral colorants to decorate ware which already has been glazed fired. Overglazes have a lower firing range than underglazes and are not as durable. The low firing range makes possible a large variety of beautiful colors.

Oxidation—Adequate mixture of air with fuel in firing to cause complete combustion.

Reduction—Reducing the amount of oxygen in the firing to produce a smoky atmosphere in the kiln.

Separator—A substance used in mold making to prevent the plaster from adhering wherever separation is desired.

Sgraffito—A design scratched through the outer layer of slip which covers a body of contrasting color, thus exposing the body color through the scratched design.

Short—A lack of plasticity in clay which feels somewhat crumbly and cracks when it is being shaped.

Slip—Clay in liquid form.

Slip tracer—A syringe-like rubber bulb with a thin nozzle used for tracing a slip design on a piece of ware.

Sodium carbonate—Used as a deflocculent in casting slip.

Sodium silicate—Water glass, used as a deflocculent in casting a slip; also used in mending biscuit-ware.

Sprig—A raised design which is cast in a mold and then attached to the ware.

Suspension—The state in which particles mixed with water are kept in equal distribution, preventing them from settling to the bottom of the container.

Throwing—Forming ware on the pottery wheel.

Turning—Trimming ware in the leather-hard state while it is being turned on the pottery wheel.

Undercut—A shape cut into the model or mold that forms a pocket in which the plaster or clay casting is grasped, making release impossible without spoiling the form.

Underglaze—Colors which can withstand high temperatures. They are used for painting designs on ware.

Vermiculite—Mica in the form of tiny flakes; sometimes used in clay mixtures to give a decorative, sparkling effect.

Viscous glaze—Thick, such as the matt glazes. Will not flow.

Vitrification—The stage at which glazes melt into a fused, glassy surface and the component particles in clay unite into a strong, dense, and glass-like substance.

Wedging—Throwing and pounding clay before it is formed, in order to drive out the air.

Index

Index